D1420533

Personnel in Change

Personnel in Change

ORGANIZATION DEVELOPMENT
THROUGH THE PERSONNEL FUNCTION

Edited by
Manab Thakur
John Bristow
Keith Carby

INSTITUTE OF PERSONNEL MANAGEMENT

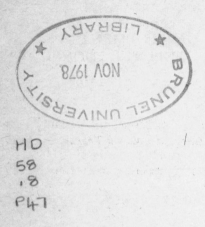
Text set in 10/12 pt VIP Garamond, printed by photolithography,
and bound in Great Britain at The Pitman Press, Bath

ISBN 0 85292 161 6

Contents

Foreword

There is a great deal of misunderstanding and apprehension about the whole subject of organizational development or OD as it is conveniently known. These doubts surrounding OD will be dispelled most readily in circumstances where it is practised effectively as a means of tackling genuine and immediate problems. Unfortunately, this has not always been the case and a disservice has sometimes been done to OD through the misapplication of concepts and techniques by those who lack real understanding of what is involved. This fact does not provide a justification for ignoring OD. On the contrary, it means that personnel specialists will be much better placed to serve their organizations when they know more of how OD may be used to help set and achieve organizational objectives.

In this rapidly changing business world it is imperative that the executive, whatever his discipline, should give consideration to the principles and practices of OD. There are many publications on OD available to help in this but few deal with the subject in such a clear and precise way as is the case here. The book is even more unusual in that it represents a pioneering attempt to relate OD ideas and practices to the normal functions of personnel. It is very much a practitioners' book and this orientation should enable the reader more easily to consider OD in terms of his or her own circumstances.

I believe *Personnel in Change* is aptly timed as a valuable book for the personnel executive in particular. It presents the ideas and tools of OD in a way which will show personnel specialists how they can extend the resources they are able to offer towards helping an organization meet the many challenges that face the modern enterprise.

Managing Director
Scottish Industries Training and Management Services
Vice-President-Training and Development IPM

Preface

The main title of this book may be given at least two interpretations. *Personnel in Change* could refer to the role of the personnel function in an environment of change. Equally, it might relate to a transformation in the way the personnel function operates (we include training as a vital part of the personnel function). The sub-title, *Organization development through the personnel function* is more specific in describing the nature of the book's content but the ambiguity in the main title is not accidental. Our primary purpose is to show the ways in which the personnel function can help an organization adapt to change and plan its own development. However, for this to happen, there is little doubt that the knowledge and skills used by personnel specialists in carrying out their traditional organizational roles will need to be extended.

Organization development (OD), which is a multi-disciplinary approach to planned change, is not the sole preserve of the personnel function. Nevertheless we believe that if OD is to gain acceptance and become a widely used practical tool, the personnel function will have to understand and practice it. The need for more widespread efforts to translate OD into action is greater (and the demands made in applying it are higher) because it is an integrated set of concepts and not just a collection of techniques. In order to be of value and to be widely recognized as such, these concepts need to be translated in terms of day to day organizational activities. The rewards for achieving this are likely to be higher, as the unique features of each organization mean that the uncritical application of techniques alone will generally be of limited value. The purpose of the book is to show how OD can be practised in relation to specific functions of personnel management. We believe that personnel managers, training managers and others will gain from the opportunity of examining examples of the contribution that OD can make to the personnel aspects of organizational life.

The material should be of interest irrespective of the reader's previous experience of the theory or practice of OD. For those who are newcomers to OD, chapter 1 provides an introduction to the subject. It differs from the later contributions in that it is to some extent theoretical. This is inevitable since it discusses ideas on organization in isolation from specific circumstances or problems. Chapters 2 and 3 focus respectively on the role of the personnel function in a changing environment and the introduction of OD to the organization. Some of the functional areas essential to personnel management are described in chapter 4 in terms of the contribution OD can make towards their development. We do not suggest that the areas omitted are of no significance but the limitations on space made some selection inevitable. Chapter 5 contains case studies of organization development.

Some short biographical notes on each of our authors are given on page 150 at the end of the book. We are deeply indebted to each of these people for their contributions. Our sincere thanks are also due to several members of the British OD network and to Frances Rammage, of Philips Industries, who helped in the preparatory stages and to Jenny Blake, Independent Consultant, Peter Burger, Social Ecology Associates, Chris Hayes, Training Services Agency and Philip Sadler and Peter Smith, both of Ashridge Management College, for providing valuable comments. We are also grateful to Tom Jaap for providing a foreword to our efforts.

The assistance of all these people has been invaluable. They share no responsibility, however, for any inadequacies or limitations of the final text.

Manab Thakur
John Bristow
Keith Carby
London, November 1977

CHAPTER I

An introduction to organization development (OD)

John Bristow, Keith Carby and Manab Thakur

The number and severity of present day problems surrounding employment mean that the personnel function is placed in a crucial and demanding role. While many of the policy decisions on major issues such as pay, productivity and participation may be made elsewhere it will usually be the personnel department which will be primarily involved in helping the organization cope with changes in these and similar areas. The erosion of supervisors' authority, extensive and involved employment legislation, frustration over differentials and the problems associated with management unionization are just a few of the specific dilemmas now facing personnel specialists. Responses to these challenges which consist of a series of haphazard adaptations are unlikely to increase the effectiveness of an organization or help it in the long term struggle to survive successfully in a changing environment. Progress of this kind is more likely to be achieved when each new challenge is treated as an opportunity for development.

The abbreviation OD refers to an integrated set of ideas which together offer both a direction for development of the organization and some means by which it may be realized. It is essential therefore that the concepts and values embodied by OD should be discussed and then tried out in practice on as wide a basis as possible. Unfortunately, many of the short definitions of OD tend to do little to bring about this diffusion. Such descriptions often say in unfamiliar language that OD is about using behavioural science knowledge, managing planned change and increasing the 'health' of organizations. It is not surprising that many readers are still left wondering what OD really is and whether it could be of use to them. In this first chapter, we eschew short definitions in favour of a gradual and more extensive introduction to OD. We begin in Part 1 with a brief review of the need for OD. A picture of what OD might look like in action is then given by showing the sort of differences it would make to organizations: differences which would signify a development in the way people work together. In Part 2 we take the definition of OD further by outlining a process for development and by

1

describing the strategic principles and techniques that can be used to help organizations move through it.

PART 1   A PICTURE OF DEVELOPMENT

THE NEED FOR OD

The tendency for modern organizations to be large and the fast changing and complex environment in which all organizations must operate are two of the major characteristics of the age in which we live.

Increase in size usually means increases in organizational problems. This is not to say 'small is beautiful' in every way. Smaller organizations also have their developmental problems. They may be strongly affected by single personalities and they may suffer from narrowness, exploitation or the stubborness of their owners or managers about change of any kind. Nevertheless, smaller organizations are less affected by some of the disadvantages which increase in intensity as the enterprise grows larger. For example, the small organization's goals are likely to be clearer and better understood by the people in that organization. Control may be exercised on a personal, human basis and everyone can better identify with and participate in producing the goods or services of the organization. People in small organizations are also more likely to have direct contact with customers and clients and they will usually have more freedom and flexibility of role. This will show itself in the amount of initiative and improvisation they are able to bring to their work and the amount of satisfaction they can derive from it.

As the size of the organization increases (usually for reasons of economy of scale and by means of technological advances) these advantages become progressively harder to maintain. The basis of ordering and controlling effort changes. It becomes more difficult to 'hold the organization together' and there is a tendency for it to become rationalized rather than intuitive, impersonal rather than personal and so mechanical rather than organic. Communication has to be ordered through channels or networks. Also, tasks and roles become routine, specialized and separated from each other and, as a result, they have to be co-ordinated through a technical system or supervisor. The organization grows more prone to many other ills as it grows in size. For example, interdepartmental rivalries may occur, and confusion and misunderstanding over objectives and tasks tend to become more frequent. People at the 'bottom' of the organization may not have an appreciation of the overall picture and they may be less likely to see the actions of 'top' management as benign or intelligent. Management of the organization increasingly feels it has to control closely and direct precisely all those below, and as communication between the two becomes

2

less effective the scene is set for a hardening of attitudes which may prove disruptive. All this can result in a lack of commitment to the organization and its work, and a sense of isolation, meaninglessness and alienation throughout the workforce.

Despite these disadvantages, large organizations are a fact of life and there is little doubt that they are here to stay for the foreseeable future. Thanks to modern technology, advanced means of communication and the economic system itself, these organizations can operate adequately but often well below their real potential. There is little doubt that we have yet to learn how co-ordination, communication and control can take place in large organizations so that the advantages of the small organization are not lost, so that people can feel truly involved in their work and so that high levels of performance can be consistently maintained.

Perhaps the most striking feature of modern times is the staggering rate at which change occurs. This has been adequately documented elsewhere[1]* and much has also been written about the impact it has on organizations.[2] The modern enterprise is constantly faced with new challenges and over the last few years no organization can have remained unchanged in the face of technological advances, shifts in markets, inflation, the boom in oil prices, employment legislation, ecological restrictions on growth, the expansion of knowledge and specialization and many other factors.

In addition to economic, technological and political change, organizations have had to adapt to new values and aspirations in society. The extension of education leads school leavers to expect more of their working life. Changing attitudes towards authority at school, at home and at the workplace have put pressure on management to exercise its authority differently. All in all, the environment is more complex and interdependent and subject to fundamental change at an unprecedented rate. There is no doubt that:

> As the rate of change of so many environmental variables increases, it is no longer very likely that the 'perfect' organization can be created to do a particular set of tasks indefinitely. The tasks change, available workers change in their attitudes and motivations and so on. Structures and policies that were excellent when created can quickly become outdated and harmful to the long-term survival of the system. The organization needs to have conscious procedures for adapting and re-shaping itself.[3]

OD offers a way by which organizations can build in a 'self-renewing' capability. This helps not only to conserve 'stability in the face of recurring disintegrative pressures from the environment',[4] it can also assist an organization, whatever its size, to improve on its level of effectiveness.

* All numbered references are listed on page 153.

THE NATURE OF DEVELOPMENT

An organization is, in simple terms, a number of people working together in some setting to achieve certain goals. As an organization develops, the quality of this communal effort is transformed. Development, as OD defines it, occurs when the people working together take on new values, new behaviour and new understanding which are more relevant in the light of their own needs, those of the organization and the pressures brought to bear by the environment which surrounds them. This distinguishes development from change. Change by itself may be in structures or 'appearances' only. For example, a change may be the movement of a machine, an alteration in shifts, the enlarging of jobs or the introduction of a new agreement on manning. These changes may be the signal for development but they are not themselves developments in the sense in which the word is used in OD. Development involves transformations in culture. The qualitative nature of development also distinguishes it from growth which is merely an increase in size.

We are aware of the well-known risk of describing how development is defined in OD. The definition of development embraces certain ideals and the translation of these into an ideal picture gives an image which is so far away from present practice that some people tend immediately to condemn it as naive and totally unrealizable. To do this is to miss the point. **These ideals are laid down in order to give a sense of direction for development efforts.** They are not presented as something which must or can be realized immediately. It is important to remember this when viewing the following examples of what changes might occur in an organization as it 'develops'. Changes can take place in:

1 The way goals are set, decisions are made, and work is organized and controlled; that is, changes will occur in the distribution and balance of power
2 The quality of work relationships between people and groups
3 The role and style of management
4 The characteristics of the overall structure and the way it is determined
5 The quality and degree of integration of individuals and groups within the organization
6 The ability of the organization to learn from experience and to relate to its environment and the future
7 The manner in which people as individuals are encouraged and helped to develop.

The following are short descriptions of what development might mean in each of these areas. The assumptions and values implicit in these descriptions characterize OD.

4

1 Control and decision making

OD sets out to invite members of the organization to invest freely their intelligence and energy in their work. The *aim* is self-reliant and responsible functioning on the part of all with ever greater degrees of self-organization shown by employees. As progress towards this goal is achieved control may be exercised more through commitment and through teamwork than by the use of hierarchies, rules and incentives. For this to happen people will need to know how their efforts fit in with the work of the whole organization and they will have an influence in the decision making process.

If decision making is based on the exchange of relevant and valid information, decisions will be of a higher quality. This means that they will also be made by those with the appropriate data and competence and not just by those who occupy a particular status or position. The people to be involved in a particular decision can be determined on the basis of factors and constraints such as time, cost and the likely impact of the decision on employees' working lives. It is possible for policies to be modified through feedback from all parts of the organization and this process should mean that they are more effective. Decisions about the distribution of wealth are made through a negotiation process in which information is more openly disclosed. OD does not prescribe any form of decision-making and control. It emphasizes the benefits of working through the underlying values and their implications in relation to tasks, the environment and the capacities and inclinations of the people involved.

2 The quality of working relationships

If individuals in the organization are to achieve and maintain higher self-reliance, the social relationships they form at work will need to facilitate rather than impair this development. People and groups can learn how to build recognition of interdependence and show a higher level of mutual trust. With trust, communication between people can be more open and free-flowing so that the quality of functioning may be improved and effectiveness generally increased. This is difficult to achieve because it will mean that people must *learn* how to create interdependent relationships and trust. Such a condition cannot be artificially imposed or constructed. It must be fostered—continuously.

Conflict is virtually endemic in organizations and can either be disruptive or creative. For conflict to be creative it must be worked through by confronting and exploring issues, and by problem-solving and negotiating. It can then improve the quality of decision-making and enable greater social integration to occur. If it is smoothed over, avoided, suppressed, increased, exploited or manipulated the penalties that result from such strategies can be severe. There are different sources and types of conflict and people need to learn to recognize, understand and handle these accordingly. Conflict occurs between individuals

5

and groups throughout the organization, no matter what their role. It is not confined to the management–union dialogue. At all levels the developing organization builds up appropriate structures, norms and competence to handle the different kinds of conflict.

3   The role and style of management

As an organization develops, management increasingly recognizes the importance of fostering human resources. There is a greater concern to give people the confidence and ability to take on responsibility and to encourage them of their own free will to pursue greater effectiveness and satisfaction at work. Managers themselves will be given greater recognition for developing their staff. Appraisals, providing feedback on performance and learning on-the-job become higher priorities.

Another possible indicator of development might be the existence of social policies on the organization's human resources and relations with the environment. These will be an integral part of corporate planning. Manpower planning can then be more meaningful and, if practised in an open and collaborative manner, it can contribute significantly to the organization's economic and social performance.

With the growth of self-organization and greater commitment on the part of employees, managers can feel freer to change their style of leadership. Development means that management has to adapt its style to meet existing needs, using a participative rather than an autocratic framework.

Management is also encouraged to think of the organization as an 'open system'. This means treating the organization and each constituent part as 'an organism which trades with its environment—importing inputs, transforming them and exporting a product (person, thing, idea or energy) to the environment'.[5] Thinking in this way enables management to get a firmer grasp of complex phenomena and allows managers to see how the various parts of the organization fit together—markets, production processes and the social system. The kind of attention and value given to each part may well change through this type of approach. 'Systems thinking' also helps managers to scan, identify and relate to their environment and so can lead to a greater orientation to the future.

4   The form of organizational structure

In the developing organization structure tends to be determined consciously by those involved with a view to increasing effectiveness rather than solely for reasons of control. The task in hand determines structure and the structure grows more flexible and adaptable. This need not inevitably cause confusion as the system of working roles can be better integrated if role incumbents have a clearer understanding of their part in the organization's operations. Through

6

this awareness of the interrelationship between roles people are better placed to revise the structure in which they operate.

The formation of both vertical and lateral structural relationships is another pointer to development. Better vertical relationships mean that policy formation is more closely integrated with implementation. Teamwork is fostered through sounder horizontal relationships. In this way the 'connective tissue' of the organization is strengthened. One of the consequences of this is likely to be the blurring of the distinction between staff and line personnel. Also, responsibilities will be shared more, though individual roles will be retained.

Development may well be accompanied by the organization becoming a federation of sub-organizations and communities with power being appropriately distributed throughout these subsidiary units. Other structural changes are likely to be a reduction in the number of levels of management, a move towards smaller functional units and alterations in the reward system. Pay and status will become *less* important as incentives and this will mean a structural change in that unnecessary differences will gradually disappear.

5 The level of integration

The word integration as it is used here relates to the degree to which people share values, norms and goals. OD aims for greater integration in the belief that this will result in employees having a different kind of contract with the organization, one that is based more on a sense of involvement than on the necessity to take employment in the organization solely in order to satisfy basic needs. In this situation participation can be more meaningful, with people identifying with the team and the working community rather than being 'just a cog in the machine'.

Greater integration does not mean a lack of diversity throughout the organization. For example, in larger organizations there are bound to be differences in goals and values across functions such as finance, production, marketing and personnel. There will be a need for appropriate structural links which allow for the constructive use of this conflict.

6 The adaptability of the organization and its relations with the environment

It is important for every organization to realize that ultimately, it depends on a wider environment (both society and nature) for support and survival. Unless it is responsible in both its attitudes and behaviour the support may be withdrawn or the resources may no longer be available. The developing organization is more open to its surroundings, while maintaining its stability, and shows in all its policies and operations that it sees itself as having a dynamic relationship with that environment. The organization's surroundings are continually monitored for changes and when these are sensed they are confronted and analysed. This enables a proactive and planned approach to be taken so that sudden reactions and crises are *less* likely. As Robert Townsend so graphically put it, 'Good organizations are living bodies that grow muscles to meet changes.'[6]

The developing organization therefore becomes more adaptable. It seeks to be in touch with the needs of its customers and tries to adjust to their changing requirements. Profit and its distribution to shareholders remain part of the organization's 'mission' (its range of objectives) but they become a means rather than an end. Good profits maintain and develop the business, provide rewards and security for members and resources for development activities.

7 *Individual and group development*

Organization development cannot occur without the development of groups and individuals. The way this is done will be related to the culture of the organization and to the society to which the organization belongs. Thus the focus of individual development will be different according to the people, the situation and the time. The OD approach to individual development is based on the assumption that it would be beneficial if people could become freer of defensive behaviour, dependency or a narrow self-orientation; grow more open to experience, including feelings; be more able to learn from these experiences and build up confidence and autonomy. It is assumed that people *can* grow richer in these attributes. A fundamental aspect of the OD approach to individual development is the contention that the 'whole man' is involved in development. In other words an employee's personal feelings, needs and values have to be considered just as much as any skills and knowledge which are directly related to the job. At any one moment the focus of an individual's development will have to be related to a specific situation or question. However, although the context may be one of work, distinctions between professional or management development and individual development are conceptual only and, in some cases, artificial.

In a developing organization, some understanding of individual development, and the challenge and opportunities in life that can be its spur, will become part of the organizational culture. In the same way understanding of how groups or teams can be formed and fostered will be built up and there will be a greater appreciation of the necessary conditions for this and how these may be created.

IS DEVELOPMENT POSSIBLE?

As we emphasized earlier, this description of development given here is meant to awaken a sense of values and to help find a direction for the future. There is no suggestion that every organization could and should immediately have a highly responsible and self-organizing workforce or that each enterprise can immediately become totally participative, integrated and self-adapting. Nevertheless, we would suggest that there is no doubt that the ideas on development intrinsic to OD are of real value at present. Means have been devised by which these ideas may be pursued in practice. These are illustrated in part 2 of this chapter and the rest of the book is almost exclusively concerned with OD in action. This material shows clearly that OD in practice starts with realities and there is no attempt to follow blindly a set of academic theories or ideals. However, it is the tension between 'what is' and 'what is desired' that provides the orientation and very often the energy for developmental activities.

Some managers have a negative initial response to the way development is defined in OD. They may feel that the general direction intrinsic to OD is laudable and the way we ought to be progressing but that, sadly, it is impossible to follow such a course in practice. Other managers may disagree with the underlying values and assumptions. Much of the scepticism concerning OD comes from managers who basically take a very negative view of the attitudes and motives held by people at work. They see employees in what McGregor termed, the 'Theory X'[7] way. This is the traditional view of direction and control in organizations whereby it is assumed that the average human being has an inherent dislike of work, needs to be coerced, controlled, directed and threatened in order to achieve objectives and that he prefers to avoid responsibility in favour of being directed by others. This outlook can be a self-fulfilling prophecy as, when conditioned by these beliefs, organizations may develop control systems, reward structures and so on, which encourage just those irresponsible behaviours that were predicted. In other words the attitudes and relationships that some managers cite as showing development to be impossible might have been created by their own beliefs and behaviour.

Progress throughout society as a whole has rendered the Theory X approach generally less appropriate and also much less effective. This is especially so when there is a need for organizational change:

> Given the nature of social systems in the modern organizational world the command/obedience style of management is less and less appropriate to changing an organization since research shows that this style has a high probability of producing unintended consequences that are often inimical to the goals of change.[8]

There are indications that the benefits of a participative approach are being increasingly recognized as more experience of it is gained. For example, the attitude of Japanese top management on this subject was recently summarized as follows:

It has become clear to us that organizations supported by free-flowing information and by responsible judgement and actions on the part of every one of their members are lively organizations, without any confusion or chaos to disturb their order. They represent genuinely creative organizations, firmly based on effective communication and identification with the company through the self-realization it affords.[9]

There is no doubt that development will rarely be easy. People invariably meet resistance to change when it is first encountered in themselves or in others. They may cope with the stresses accompanying change by showing inertia, apathy, fear or outright hostility. If development is to occur, these responses will need to be confronted and worked through. There is no short cut. However, people cannot be forced to do this. Genuine development of individuals and groups can only take place through choice and acceptance.

Thinking in terms of stages of development can help dislodge any fixation on an idealist picture. It can also indicate where attention might best be focused and where a strategy for further development can be devised which is more easily manageable and attainable. For example, it might be that a relatively poorly developed organization contains pockets or units which are more participative and consultative in their leadership. There may therefore be an opportunity to take this development a stage further by encouraging teamwork and collaborative forms of direction and control. Success in this unit will almost certainly have a beneficial (although not always immediate) effect on the rest of the organization.

When describing the organization or any part of it in terms of relative stages of development it should be borne in mind that an organization can never be said to have 'arrived'. OD is an activity that is conducted continuously. In this way an organization can not only accommodate new social, ecological, economic and technological pressures, it can use many of these stimuli to strengthen itself and enhance its operations.

PART 2   ACHIEVING ORGANIZATIONAL DEVELOPMENT

Having now described what development might look like, and having briefly noted some of the needs and constraints which respectively act for and against it, the second half of this chapter deals with how development may be achieved using strategies and techniques derived from the ideas and principles fundamental to OD.

ORIGINS OF OD

A very short description of the origins of OD is given here as it shows the concepts and experiences which were drawn together in the search to find practicable tools which could be used to develop organizations. Each of the major contributions is only briefly mentioned but the references provided can be consulted by those who wish to read more about any particular input.

OD did not emerge from a single event at any one moment. It took shape gradually as different elements were brought together from disparate sources over several years. It is widely accepted, however, that the emergence of OD was signalled in the 1930s in the USA when a need for finding new methods of increasing organizational effectiveness was already being expressed. The traditional approach to improving organizational performance (which is still much in evidence) was believed to have several weaknesses. This traditional approach was based on the continuous use of training and development courses or programmes for individuals whilst one-off interventions, often made with the assistance of outside 'expert' consultants, were used to tackle specific organizational problems and to promote greater overall effectiveness. In the case of the latter the consultants, who invariably worked within closely defined terms of reference, would write a report and make recommendations based on their study of the situation. If these recommendations called for changes in the organization they would then (if supported by top management) be implemented using the existing authority structure of the organization.

A growing number of people began to voice doubts as to the effectiveness of the approaches both to individual and to organizational development. There was evidence from practical experience and from research that individual training did not transfer sufficiently well to the workplace. It was also believed that recommendations set out in a report to top management, even when based on diligent and exhaustive diagnosis, rarely resulted in the achievement of substantial progress. As a result, the new findings emerging from the social sciences were used in order to form a different and more effective means of 'social consultancy'.

Perhaps the most significant early breakthrough stemmed from the now-famous Hawthorne studies done by Elton Mayo[10] and others in Chicago in the 1930s. This work greatly increased awareness of how the quality of human relations could influence performance in organizations. In 1947 Kurt Lewin[11] and other social psychologists formed what is now the National Training Laboratories of Applied Behavioural Science (NTL) at Bethel, Maine, in the USA. The NTL provided a focus for a dramatic surge of innovative thinking and new ideas on the theory of change, group dynamics and 'action research'. The NTL was principally responsible for using and promoting T-groups[12] as a means of human relations training in employment based on intense, self-analytical experience in small groups.

The ideas and work of several other individuals and institutions played a part in progressing the formulation of OD. The theories of John Dewey,[13] an American educational philosopher, were used. In particular, his emphasis on problem-solving as a fundamental process in all learning was a formative influence. The work of Carl Rogers[14] in individual and group psychotherapy led to the concept of 'client-centred' helping and change and this also was assimilated. Another major contributor was Argyris[15] who outlined the concept of interpersonal competence and discussed theories of intervening in organizations.

Some of the new ideas from the behavioural sciences were first applied in a management context by Douglas McGregor[16] who, using Maslow's[17] theories on motivation, proposed a new philosophy of management. This assumed (as opposed to theory X) that people could be trusted and allowed to use their own initiative at work. They did not need to be autocratically controlled or driven solely by 'sticks and carrots' in order to perform their tasks satisfactorily. Support for this Theory Y approach came from many quarters but perhaps most notably from Rensis Likert's[18] research into organizational effectiveness.

Another major influence in the evolution of OD was the growth in understanding of 'systems theory'[19] which was used in biology and then sociology. Systems theory was applied in the context of work by members of the Tavistock Institute of Human Relations in the UK. They developed a 'socio–technical'[20] systems approach (based on the belief that an 'organization must be regarded not solely as a technical system, nor as a social system, but as a joint socio–technical system'[21]). This considerably furthered understanding of how organizations function. Lawrence and Lorsch,[22] amongst others, were prominent in advancing theoretical appreciation of aspects of organizational structure and design. The works of Beckhard,[23] Bennis,[24] and Schein[25] and several others heralded the growing maturity of OD by demonstrating how behavioural science could be practically applied in organizations. At the same time Lievegoed[26] in Holland made a significant contribution when he described phases of development experienced by organizations and showed ways in which people could develop when working together.

A PROCESS FOR DEVELOPMENT

As more knowledge and experience of managing change in organizations was accumulated an understanding emerged of a process through which development could be achieved. The following is a description of that process and its constituent phases:

A *need*

The cycle of development starts with some pressure for change and the sensing of a need for development by members (usually but not always leading members) of the organization. This 'trigger' can consist of:

> (An) awareness of some discrepancy between expected and desired outcome (goals) and actual results. We usually think of this as a way of spotting trouble when the results are on the low side. However, it is just as much a way of locating *unanticipated opportunities* when results are on the high side.[27]

Thus the impetus for development need not come from problems alone. However, the need for development will first be appreciated when, for instance, someone senses that the many good ideas of the design department rarely result in marketable products, that the quality of work in a particular area is too low, that some managers are making decisions on the basis of inadequate information, or that the organization is failing to recruit and retain a particular type of employee. It is problems such as these which will invariably be at least part of the stimulus for development. To look for problems merely to fit an OD activity would be to reduce it to a game.

Seeking help

It can be extremely difficult for an organization to achieve development without the involvement of a 'third party' who will be given specific responsibility for facilitating progress:

> It has been found that people whose whole cultural experience has been an education in the rightness of the command/obedience style can rarely make significant modifications in their behaviour to find new adaptive relations with their organization without the help of third parties who are professionally trained to give this kind of help.[28]

If there is no one inside the organization who can fulfil this role of 'internal consultant' or 'change agent', it will be necessary to bring someone from outside. This may be unavoidable if the organization lacks anyone with the necessary training and experience to do the job. It might also be desirable because of the relative 'neutrality' of an outsider. A change agent from outside the organization will be usually less constrained by any organizational politics and 'conditioning':

> This may be related to the aura created by an external (often highly paid) consultant but it is equally related to the ability of the external change agent to 'see' with more innocence and clarity the problem which insiders may have long learned to avoid or overlook and most certainly regard with anxiety.[29]

If it is decided that an outside consultant should be employed it is a good idea to ask the person concerned to visit the organization to talk about his or her conceptual framework, approach to development, modes of operation and the means by which he or she would tackle the project at hand. This can be done without commitment and it allows the relevant members of the organization (and where necessary the unions), to get acquainted with the change agent prior to any formal arrangement being drawn up. If the consultant finds general acceptance, the organization can then work out a contract of mutual expectations with the consultant, specifying the nature of the projected relationship, its goals and procedures.[30]

Whether the change agent is from within or outside the organization, his role will be that of a facilitator of change, learning and developing rather than an expert giving advice. He or she will frequently play the part of a 'process consultant'. Process consultation is:

a set of activities on the part of the consultant which help the client to perceive, understand and act upon process events which occur in the client's environment. The process consultant seeks to give the client 'insight' into what is going on around him, within him and between him and other people. The events to be observed and learned from are primarily the various human actions which occur in the normal flow of work, in the conduct of meetings and in formal or informal encounters between members of the organization. Of particular relevance are the client's own actions and their impact on other people.[31]

Thus the process consultant needs to be 'an expert on processes at the individual, interpersonal and intergroup levels'.[32] The OD consultant will of course need additional skills and knowledge about organizational processes other than the human ones (production, financial, marketing and so on). He or she will also need to be aware of any personal needs and interests (such as to achieve acceptance, influence or success) and values (about power or structure). Usually, these are best declared from the outset. The consultant can do his or her work most effectively when he or she is accepted by all relevant interest groups. The ability to establish trust and credibility on an organization-wide basis is therefore a fundamental attribute.

Diagnosis
The first stage of any OD work is diagnosis. The consultant, working with others in the organization may use a wide variety of methods for gathering data. These might include observation, workshops, conferences and interviews as well as more formal questionnaires. The consultant's goal will be the formulation of a

joint diagnosis which can be arrived at as a result of 'feeding back' information to the relevant individuals and groups. This part of the process may involve a fair degree of conflict and the consultant will often have to work hard to encourage people to confront realities and talk through the emotional issues involved. The desired outcome is a widely shared appreciation of the realities of the situation and a common belief in the need to seek improvement.

Finding a direction

As a result of the diagnosis it should be possible for goals to be set and for a direction for the future to be identified. It is essential that the values implied by these goals should be questioned and clarified. Failure to work through differences in values exposes the organization to the risk of the changes being cosmetic only. They will therefore fail to meet the fundamental needs of the organization. The employment of an experienced change agent should ensure that this vital review is not omitted. Involving all relevant interest groups should also mean that the values implicit to the chosen course of action are thoroughly examined. The change agent can also play a useful role at this point by introducing new ideas which could help the various individuals and groups to see what development might look like in any particular situation.

Once a direction has been found and thoroughly reviewed a precise plan of action can be devised. This will mean finding answers to questions such as:

> Who are the people who are motivated to make a change attempt? What are their points of influence and leverage on the system? What variables can they most readily affect? The answers to these questions can guide a search for several alternative plans which show promise of altering the performance of the system in a desired direction.[33]

At the end of this phase a fuller appreciation of the future should exist and a statement of intent on the future should emerge.

Development activity

There are many different forms of development activities which may be used. (These are discussed in more detail later.) The choice will depend on the focus agreed for the activity—for example, on policies, roles, building relationships, structures or on learning and training. There will usually be a need in the early stages to undertake activities which are meant to 'unfreeze' areas of the organization so that change may take place. These may take the form of training exercises in communication skills and group functioning. It is a distinctive feature of OD that both diagnosis and change activities include an emphasis on the 'here and now' aspects of individuals and group behaviour. Concepts and techniques drawn from the social sciences may be used for seeing, understanding and evaluating these aspects. These may be concomitant with the setting up of relevant tasks and projects for groups or individuals. Such tasks help to engage commitment, focus energies and forge relationships which will all prove of value in securing results relevant to the organization's objectives.

The focus of development activities may well change over time. For instance, it is common for changes in roles and structure to follow and be an expression of changes in attitudes, relationships and understanding. The actual sequence and the types of activities will depend on the extent of a need and on the degree of readiness for change. Thus they will depend on, for example, the degree of trust and support that exists or needs to be built up between individuals and groups in order for them to communicate and face realities, and the strength of leadership and the support given or needed from top management.

Evaluation and review

The final phase of the development sequence is evaluation. This phase provides further learning as the outcome of the development activities are discussed and analysed. Often the success of any programme can be assessed in terms of the extent to which key individuals in the organization have gained in knowledge and experience of organizational improvement so that they are better equipped to initiate and carry out future developmental efforts themselves. Some of the other results of OD might be a change in the way work is controlled, organized and rewarded; the existence of greater trust and openness in both conflict and collaborative situations; an ability on the part of individuals and groups to learn and develop through facing difficulties; an understanding of how structures may be changed; clearer goals and policies; and greater awareness of the values and assumptions underlying management.

Continuous cycles of development

If an organization is to maintain a self-renewing capability, OD efforts will need to be continuous. At the end of each cycle of development subsequent steps can be planned on the basis of the evaluation carried out. Each new situation may be reviewed as it arises and development therefore takes place as a continuous series of discrete events rather than as a grand programme or campaign. It usually proves counterproductive to force change and each situation will need to be assessed for the appropriate depth, spread and pace of change. The process of change:

> is not a simple linear sequence. Change initiatives occur on several fronts at once. Resistance and sticking points occur on all these fronts. Some thrusts occur quickly and easily, while others seem to occur with glacial slowness. Unexpectedly, the system may appear to revert to tried-and-true methods

even though everyone agrees that these are bankrupt and discredited ways of doing business.[34]

STRATEGIC PRINCIPLES

The educational strategies which are drawn up by OD practitioners to take an organization through each cycle of development are usually based on certain operating principles. These are derived from an understanding of the conditions necessary for movement through each stage of this cycle. Here are some of the most fundamental:

Motivation and choice

Development can only be effectively achieved when a real need for change exists. People must be left free to choose—'The basic value underlying all organization theory and practice is that of choice.'[35] It is possible and often necessary for a need to be aroused in people by providing them with feedback on the difference between what is and what is desired. This can lead to an unfreezing in which they come to understand, accept and commit themselves to change based on their own values and goals, their own sense of need and their own judgement of what is possible.

Participation and responsibility

People will generally support what they create themselves and resist any changes which they feel to be alien to them. It is therefore preferable whenever possible for the employees affected, or at least their representatives, to participate in fact-finding, goal-setting and planning so that they 'own' the changes and are more committed to them. In order for people to participate effectively they need to be given the relevant information.

Beginning with diagnosis

OD starts with fact-finding. This means an objective assessment of all aspects of the organization's performance—technical, economic and social. The resulting strategies for intervention will be based on this diagnosis and will be tailor-made to the culture of the organization, its needs, constraints and readiness for change.

Small groups

Small groups provide a most effective means of transforming the performance of an organization. They tend to provide support during the process of change and help individuals to attain new values, norms and role relationships. New social ties formed during a change process are naturally accompanied by changes in attitude and behaviour. People tend to change together. Small group work during a change can also begin to establish a team approach leading to more adaptive, sensitive and intelligent social units interrelating to form a whole organization.

Focus on the whole system; tasks, relationships and structure

Human development in individuals and in organizations occurs both in relation to others in the social system or sub-system *and* in relation to the task or technical and economic system. Changes in the social system affect the economic and technical system and vice versa. For example, the introduction of new machinery may require different manning levels to be negotiated and skills to be learnt. New people may have to be recruited and new relationships will be formed.

Different ways of supervising, checking and scheduling the work may be called for. All this may result in individuals feeling and acting differently towards their jobs, their workmates and the organization. OD focuses on the whole system in the knowledge that any change in any area of the organization will have repercussive effects elsewhere in the system.

It is sometimes wrongly suggested that OD is concerned solely with human relationships. There is no doubt that OD practitioners have helped to create a greater awareness of how the quality of human relationships affects organizational effectiveness. It is regarded as essential, however, in OD *both* to see that perceptions and feelings are shared through feedback so as to bring issues to the surface *and* to set up better structures and task processes.

An emphasis on learning and feedback

OD is fundamentally a learning process that comes about through attempting to resolve task, organizational and human issues. The aim of OD is not just to bring about the transformation of individuals, groups and organizations but rather to get each of these social units to learn how to develop themselves in their work. The change agent is therefore a guide and an educator rather than a trainer. He or she does not force certain views on others but tries to help those concerned to identify, understand and face up to their own problems and opportunities and find their own directions. In this way an organization can become more self-renewing and adaptable.

Learning has to be based on experience and related to real needs. The learning methods used in OD centre on the sequence of diagnosis, feeding back of information, evaluation and review. People can be helped to experience the effect of their own behaviour on others through receiving feedback of facts, thoughts and feelings. Individuals and groups may need to gain skills in giving 'non-evaluative' feedback (providing someone with information about the impact they have on others in such a way as not to imply condemnation or cause unnecessary offence and damage).

It is believed that interpersonal competence is fostered through the creation of relationships where this can occur rather than by the use of interactive skills training for individuals. When such relationships exist there is an enhanced possibility that development may occur in and between individuals, groups and organizations *at the same time*. The acquisition of other kinds of learning and competence will also accompany an OD effort, for example, a greater understanding of organization structure and how it works.

Change is planned

OD is concerned with planned change and that means in any OD programme goals will be set. These may, of course, be changed or amended in the light of further development or new circumstances. It is essential that the goals are clear and realistic to members of the organization. If this is so they can then relate the broader aims of change to specific situations that emerge so that these may be used as opportunities for development.

Power and influence

OD strategies are based on collaboration rather than coercion, power bargaining, formal authority or manipulation by group techniques. It has been found[36] that if channels of communication can be opened and authentic information exchanged, the development process can occur through collaboration between levels and functions. This implies that different levels and functions are opening themselves up to being influenced by each other. It therefore represents, in an informal sense, an equalization of power. This may mean that those in positions of power at the outset may have to take risks in order to improve human relations and organizational performance. Consequently they will need support when initiating actions for development. There is no doubt that their commitment is essential if development is to proceed through collaboration.

It is sometimes assumed that OD can only take place when conditions of 'truth and trust' exist. In other words development is only possible when people feel enough mutual support and confidence to be open with each other and to solve problems through the rational use of information.If this were so, it would not be possible in conditions where 'conflict and power' feature strongly (for example in most 'industrial relations' settings). Any of the protagonists in a conflict situation may not believe it politic to be completely open and truthful and each party will be wary of the other. In these conditions conflict itself, rather than collaboration or feedback, may be the lever of change and development. The OD approach would aim to develop the organization's capacity to handle

19

conflict. At the same time the distribution of power would be influenced by training people to be representatives and by the negotiation of structures for representation, governance and control.

WAYS OF ACHIEVING DEVELOPMENT

The strategic principles embraced by OD provide guidelines for the design and implementation of activities (often called 'interventions') which are meant to foster development. Interventions differ according to the *type of problem* addressed (poor communication, excessive conflict, inadequate leadership, etc.), *the size of the social unit* (individual, group, intergroup, organization) and the *method* chosen (survey feedback, process consultation, training, structural redesign, etc.). The following are brief descriptions of some of the more common modes of intervention:

1   Team building

This activity aims to improve the effectiveness of a group's work procedures and inter-personal relations. Particular attention is paid to the role of a team's leader and how he relates with his team members as well as to the roles, norms and communications patterns of the group as a whole.[37] Team building through OD can occur in many ways. The change agent might begin by carrying out a survey by interview amongst the members of the group. The data gathered in this way (on the effectiveness of procedures, the quality of working relationships, the style of the group or section leader) can then be discussed in a team workshop. Process consultation can be used to bring issues to the surface and to concentrate attention on resolving difficulties. Other methods that might be used to build teamwork are specially designed projects and training exercises which help the group examine and improve on its effectiveness.

Team building often occurs at the start of the development cycle with the top team of the social unit in question.

2   Conflict handling between individuals and groups

In this type of intervention the change agent attempts to bring out the issues underlying any conflict and to have them clarified *or* he may have to reduce the intensity of the conflict to prevent an unnecessary and destructive increase in conflict. The emphasis is placed on creating conditions which will enable the energy generated through conflict to be used constructively. The attention of a change agent before a meeting likely to involve heightened conflict would be focused on working with each of the protagonists independently (for example, man and boss or manager and shop steward). This contact allows the change agent to acquire valuable data about each side's expectations, interests,

20

attitudes, personalities and readiness to change. During the meeting the change agent will try to facilitate a reciprocal reduction in tension, developing norms and behaviour that deepen the communication, controlling or refereeing the dialogue and clarifying substantive or emotional issues. On a longer time scale the change agent will attempt to build skills and norms in the organization so that it is more capable of handling conflict. This may include counselling individuals and representatives on their own attitudes and roles. In many circumstances the change agent may offer advice to help others understand how structures, rewards and values affect the extent and type of conflict.

3 Intergroup or interdepartment sessions

Where there are distorted perceptions between two groups (for example, a production team seeing maintenance workers as slow and lazy whilst the maintenance workers see the production team as 'slap-happy' and overpaid) the OD approach might be to ask each side to compile two images—one of how they see the other group and another of how they think the other group sees them. The two groups are then brought together to exchange and discuss each other's perceptions. This helps reduce tension between the two groups and allows individuals to check their perceptions against reality.

Sometimes this is done between three groups with the members of one group looking on as relatively objective witnesses. The feedback this third group gives the other two groups can be very effective. (It is sometimes called 'organizational mirroring'). The next stage after feedback is the identification of needs and common goals. If necessary, a work team composed of members from each group can be drawn together to discuss outstanding issues and devise appropriate strategies. Such mixed teams of people from different groups or functions can be formed for intergroup goal-setting or for joint projects without going through an image exchange. Mixed teams will function more effectively if definite steps are taken to build team development across the groups. It will almost certainly be necessary for the change agent to work hard at keeping fact distinct from fiction and at preventing individuals from exerting too large an influence because of their ability to speak in meetings.

4 Confrontation meetings or organizational conferences

This mode of intervention is often used in setting change goals which more accurately match the capacities and orientations of the members of an organization or one of its constituent parts. After gathering data by survey or through interviews the change agent arranges for this to be fed back to the whole group in question. This conference then splits up into small groups consisting of people from different levels and functions in the organization in order to discuss the data. (In some cases no prior survey work may have been done, in which case these groups attempt to bring out the problems and clarify issues without the aid of systematically researched data.) When the conference re-convenes, the needs and goals identified by each of the small groups are reported and discussed. The conference then sub-divides again into functional/family groups to work on what to do. The final plenary session consists of a sharing of ideas on goals and plans so that some initial decisions can be made. It is important for the change agent to ensure that the decisions made are known and fully understood and that some people do not leave the meeting believing wrongly that ideas raised in discussion were decisions. Follow-up meetings will take place as necessary.

5 Survey feedback and action research

As can be seen from the previous descriptions most interventions involve exchange and feedback of information. Feeding back information gained from a survey is an activity which can be used by itself to start off a change process. The traditional approach to organizational surveys invariably meant collecting data from one group, which after analysis was then reported back to another group, usually senior management. In OD it is believed that 'in order to generate motivation for change, the discrepancies between organizational ideals and actual responses, as revealed by the data, must be fed back to the members who have provided the data in the first place'.[38] After that the client can then be fully involved in planning how to conduct the diagnosis. This does not imply that everyone should receive all the data collected but that those who supplied information should receive back those parts of the final body of data which are relevant to their unit or team and the role it plays in the organization. It helps a great deal if the feedback can be given in a form and language as near as possible to the way in which it was provided. Those who provided data may then assimilate the information more quickly before deciding what action to take. They may also plan their own feedback session with higher management. The change agent can help in this as well as generally providing ideas or interpretations for the 'client' group.

A related intervention to survey/feedback is action research, which is oriented more towards the future. Here the client is testing out an idea or a structure in a 'live' situation. The change agent helps the client with the research methodology associated with this kind of intervention.

6 Changing structures

OD can help in the design and implementation of both small and large scale structural change. The nature of the changes made can vary a great deal. For example, it might mean redesigning individual jobs, restructuring the work of groups or departments, re-examining the task and role of a particular committee or redesigning the technical, information and reward systems. As we have suggested already changes in structure and behaviour go hand in hand. This can be seen from the example of a structural change in which a work group is presented with the option of taking over control of the functions related to the task which were hitherto in the hands of the supervisor. Such a change would probably require members of the group to learn new tasks so as to make job rotation possible. It might also warrant training in instructing for the work group members and perhaps visits to other sections or departments with which the group comes into contact. Team building activities would probably be necessary and there would be a need to re-educate the supervisors and managers affected by the changes. It is essential to remember that in a change of this kind the work group participates in the management of the development. The new structure is not imposed on them.

A further example of how a structural intervention might occur would be a change agent assisting a board of directors to review the way it operated. This might involve the board in reassessing the way it is serviced, how frequently it meets or its tasks, procedures and composition. Yet another example might be three or four different departments or units coming together to work through their relations with each other. This might result in the establishment of new mixed function project teams or the alteration of communication and influence patterns or the inauguration of a wider debate on workflows, information flows and decision making.

On a smaller scale the change agent might help people become clearer about their own jobs and the roles of others in the organization. Where people have roles which are interdependent, this might be done by setting up a procedure for 'role negotiating' whereby there is an exchange on wants, expectations and perceptions. With more than two people, a chart might be used to display who is responsible for what and who needs to know, approve or participate in particular decisions. The aim in all this is to enable members of the organization to learn how to build and adapt roles, and how to change structures for themselves. In order to do this they will need to know the factors that determine structure, the different options available and how to set about changing structures so that they can be more openly chosen through a shared understanding of purpose.

7 *Open systems planning*

As we noted earlier, 'the notion of input–conversion–output can readily be applied to organizations in that organizations take in resources (people, raw materials, energy etc) from the environment, convert them and return them to the environment in various forms'.[39] This idea of an open system is not only applicable to relations between the organization and its environment. It also helps in understanding the operations and the interdependence of the many smaller sub-systems which exist *within* the organization.

> One sub-system's output is another's input. This is well illustrated when a sub-system ceases to function. In such a case the viability of the organization may be threatened unless it can change this sub-system or 'grow' other sub-systems to compensate. For example, financial accounting has undergone rapid changes in the past decade, yet some financial departments are too 'closed' to acknowledge this. As a result some organizations find themselves taking critical decisions on the wrong data.[40]

Thus thinking in terms of open systems provides a conceptual tool which enables people to understand how they relate to their work, the work of others and the larger environment. 'Open systems planning' is the means by which this thinking can help the organization 'as a result of seeing more of and valuing differently the complicated texture of their environments, generate a considerably more varied range of action possibilities from which to choose directions and strategies'.[41] In practice this usually takes the form of the change agent and the group concerned formulating a set of procedures which can take them through the following process:

> rapidly identify and map out the dynamic realities which are in their environment
> map out how the organization represented by the members of the group presently act toward and hence values those realities
> map out how the organization wants to engage with those realities in the future (that is, to set value goals)
> make plans to restructure the 'architecture' of the organization in order to influence the environmental realities in the valued directions.[42]

This helps to produce greater commitment. It will also promote better understanding between people by encouraging changes in attitudes towards other members of the organization and the environment. New and clearer goals should be defined and these should lead to different, more appropriate structures. Open systems planning is a process by which structures, relationships and awareness of task requirements can be evolved together.

CONCLUSION

This introductory chapter began with a brief review of why OD was needed. We discussed the problems that have tended to accompany the pronounced trend towards large-sized organizations and we pointed out how these are often exacerbated by the high rate of change which is a striking characteristic of the modern age. It was suggested that if organizations want to survive and moreover want to increase their effectiveness, they need to become more sensitive to the pressures for change and more adept at responding to these through planned development. The orientation of our description of OD has been towards illustrating how it can help organizations to meet these challenges.

We have defined OD in terms of a picture of the developing organization, a process of development and the strategic principles and activities which can be used to help organizations move through each development cycle. This description shows how OD differs from the traditional approach to the 'management of change'. Basically, it focuses on assisting individuals, groups and organizations *to learn how to develop* rather than relying on formal 'training' for individuals and seeking expert advice for organizational improvement. As we have seen, OD efforts are usually centred on groups but individual differences are taken into account. Indeed, it is believed essential that the 'whole man' should be considered; his feelings as well as his thoughts; and his relationships as well as his actions. Although there are values which are clearly implied in OD, developmental efforts always face realities squarely, moving to a view of the future and subsequently to the planning of the steps needed and feasible for achievement of the desired objectives. It questions the validity of conventional hierarchical structures and suggests options for alternative forms based on task demands. OD is multi disciplinary in that *all* aspects of an organization (economic, technical and social) are considered.

With this introduction over, the remainder of this book now concentrates on how the *personnel specialist* can help his organization develop, both as an OD internal consultant and in the more traditional personnel duties associated with the management of human resources.

CHAPTER II

The role of the personnel function in a changing environment

Brian Wilson

In this paper, Brian Wilson identifies some of the 'traps' into which the personnel function can so easily fall. He suggests that the way to develop a meaningful role for the personnel function is to start with business objectives and then to concern the top management team in thinking through the 'people implications' of running a successful enterprise.

The author discusses his involvement with a British company where he encouraged open systems thinking. This, he suggests, made the top management of the company more conscious of issues such as how people were to be used, rewarded, managed and developed. Finally, he outlines the kind of role and skills that the personnel function will need to adopt if it is to help the organization face more effectively the problems of change.

INTRODUCTION

In a world where change has become the norm, where people have changing expectations and values, in which they and their organizations are subjected to ever more pressures for change, it is essential that the personnel function should have a clear view of its own role as a facilitator of change. It must be able to help its company prepare for and manage the necessary changes with the minimum of disruption. It must also be concerned with harnessing the human energy and potential available in the best achievement of the company's goals.

All too often personnel functions are so engaged in running and maintaining their various systems and in dealing with day to day problems that they have little time to stand back and think through, in a fundamental way, the implications of the changing world and their own role.

This chapter is concerned with this kind of exploration. It is not concerned with the specific personnel contributions *per se* but rather with how these need to be carried out and co-ordinated and with the kinds of skills, insights and approaches which are necessary.

It analyses first, the ways in which personnel functions have sometimes gone wrong, why this has come about and what can be done to develop a new orientation. It then goes on to discuss some of the key emphases and skills necessary in a change-oriented dynamic function and finally discusses some of the problems likely to be encountered in bringing about the necessary changes.

THE PERSONNEL FUNCTION—THE THINGS WHICH CAN GO WRONG

Against a vision of a pro-active, diagnostic, change-orientated personnel function, which the writer believes is relevant to today's needs, this section attempts to identify some of the traps into which personnel people can so easily fall. We know there are always dangers in generalizing about symptoms of malaise. However, if what is described does not apply to your own organization, perhaps you would think about other personnel functions you have known and ask yourself whether you have not seen some of the symptoms described.

Often there is fragmentation of the various parts of the functions. A labour department or manpower services unit deals with the shop floor whilst the personnel department deals with staff. The training centre for craftsmen, operatives and supervisors is separated from management training. There is no clear link between industrial relations and management development. Organization development work is often in an entirely separate unit, despite its close interaction with all other aspects of personnel work. Each fragment tends to develop its own, cohesive value system and beliefs about the people with whom it is connected. These values are often in conflict, eg there are still considerable differences in the treatment of blue and white collar workers. It is hardly surprising therefore that units are also often in conflict or in competition. The situation is aggravated when the different units report to different directors. Until all the 'people activities' are related to an overall management philosophy which looks, in a fundamental way, at the use of people in the achievement of the organization's goals, it is not surprising that fragmentation occurs.

In dealing with people, it is important to have systems which perform smoothly and effectively. The credibility of the whole function depends upon such matters, as for example, people being paid the right amounts at the right times. Because of the need to design systems with a great deal of care and subsequently to maintain them, their purpose often becomes forgotten and the prime aim becomes to run them efficiently. As the world changes and deeper insights are gained into the impact of systems on people's behaviour, there is a need to look continually and critically at personnel systems and then to seek the

27

necessary changes. How many evaluation procedures, for example, encourage managers to build empires in order to increase the size of their jobs, when what is required is fewer numbers and higher productivity? How often is managerial attention focused on quantifiable targets to the neglect of the less quantifiable, eg development of their subordinates, because of misconceived, appraisal systems? How often is the energy of the hourly paid concentrated on 'beating the system' and maintaining their earnings with less and less productivity because of inadequate rewards structures?

True professionalism should be concerned with the evolution and development of systems as well as with their maintenance. The credibility of the function should be based on more than administrative efficiency.

Even to this day, the personnel department is sometimes used as the home for failed 'other professionals'—'Let's put him in personnel he can't do much damage there!' People transferred in this way may have little or no training and may take what for them is the easiest path, so becoming the maintainers of the systems. It is hardly surprising when this happens that the credibility of the personnel function can be very low.

As we have all probably found on our occasional visits to government or local government departments, low level officials have found that in 'running the system' they can wield considerable power. They do not wish to think; their power lies in doing it according to the rule-book! Filling the personnel function with failed 'other professionals' tends to encourage just such an emphasis on bureaucracy but there is another, more insidious pressure to move in this direction. Everyone likes to have power and influence; it is easier to have this through a bureaucratic approach than to develop it from a high personal credibility and an ability to relate to managers' problems in a very open way. To be able to do this requires an ability to cope with a considerable amount of uncertainty and risk. Often the people we put into personnel are the most structured, the ones who need the assurance of a system and set ways of doing things. The policeman's role is therefore appealing and, though some degree of policing is always necessary, the kind practised by the little bureaucrat is usually very offensive.

Managing time is a problem for all managers but particularly acute for personnel staff. Doors always have to open, telephones are always ringing. To the individual with a problem, at *that* moment it is of burning importance and he needs to speak to someone—at once. Thus to think longer-term requires particular dedication by the personnel man. If he does not make the effort he is lost. He is immediately up to his eyebrows in today's problems, putting out the fires, putting sticking plaster on the wounds and having little if any time for the preventive medicine, the anticipation and avoidance of problems, which should be a key part of his task. He often finds too that, before he realizes it, he has become the manager's Pavlovian dog—he is expected to jump, whenever required, to put out this fire or deal with that problem. All too often, too, he will find that he is doing the manager's dirty work for him, those jobs which the manager should be doing himself to meet his own responsibility in managing his own people.

The personnel man must be able to say 'No'. He must see his job more in the light of a support role, of helping his various managers do their own jobs better rather than as needing to do aspects of their jobs for them. This relates to the earlier point. If a personnel man is to take this stance he must have considerable self confidence and ability to take risks. Edmund Burke expresses this well, 'He that wrestles with us strengthens our nerves. Our antagonist is our helper.'

WHY HAS THE FUNCTION DEVELOPED IN THESE WAYS?

The natural development of the function has led to much of the fragmentation referred to. Ever since organizations moved beyond the 'man and boy' level there has been a need to recruit, reward and terminate with the inevitable demands for relevant administrative procedures. As organizations have continued to grow in size and as labour has become organized, so companies have needed to develop expertise in dealing and negotiating with the unions, establishing rates of pay, differentials, conditions of employment, disputes procedures and so on. Although not subjected to the same pressures on the staff side (these are now developing) there was still a need to develop rational rewards structures which would differentiate fairly between levels of contribution and give some basis for career development. It is interesting to note how the quite different beliefs about the two groups of employees, the blue and the white collar, probably best classified as McGregor's Theories X and Y, have led to quite different rewards/control structures. There is little trust demonstrated through the hourly-paid structures and yet, for staff, the rewards structures reflect the belief that they can be expected to be trustworthy and show initiative.

Again, growing size and specialization have led to the need to train people in the various tasks which needed to be performed. Growing union power led first of all to the formulation of craft training and this was followed by operative and supervisor training. As one might have expected, the approach to training has followed the value systems. Most of this training has tended to be didactic: 'this is the way to do it'. Although staff and management training, which tended to follow on later, has had some element of the didactic, it has increasingly been more concerned with the process of managing and has had an experiential base. Again this is consistent with Theory Y values.

In recent times, particularly post-war, the new approach to education in our schools and universities has led to different attitudes in the workforce, and increasingly to less tolerance of 'being told' at all levels. This is not only having an impact on the approach to training but, more fundamentally, on the style of management which is acceptable. Autocratic management is dying out and being replaced by 'management by consent', though the implications of this for structures, roles and work organization have still to be fully worked out. It also has a profound impact on the role and style of personnel work and the kinds of contribution which are now relevant.

This section would not be complete without reference to another rapid development, the increasing impact of legislation. There has been control for many decades now of working conditions, safety standards etc through the Factories Acts, but there has been an explosion of legislation within the last few years, with the following Acts to mention but a few now on the Statute Book: Offices, Shops and Railway Premises; Health and Safety at Work; Equal Opportunities; Sex and Race Discrimination; Employee Protection, and in all probability there will be more to come.

This increase in legislation represents an attempt by Government to bring about social justice by regulation. In many ways, this is a counter-current to much of what has already been mentioned. As people have pressed for more self-determination and autonomy, so there has been a countervailing move towards greater regulation. This presents a major pitfall to personnel people. They could attempt to meet the requirements of legislation by more and more bureaucracy, and there are already signs of this happening. It is believed that the only real way forward is through education of our managers and workforce. Though there will always be a need for some monitoring, the various requirements will only be properly met if people at all levels share the responsibility of meeting them themselves.

GETTING THE ORIENTATION RIGHT

One thing is clear: to attempt to develop a personnel management role independently of business considerations must be wrong. If this is done, much of the personnel function's work can be seen as an optional extra, something which can be one of the first candidates for cut-back when the business turns down. The only way to develop a meaningful role for the personnel function is to start with the business and to involve the top management team in thinking through the people implications of running a successful business. The work done in Shell and described in *Towards a New Philosophy of Management*, by Paul Hill, is a good illustration of this. Management was involved in a thorough-going, socio-technical analysis of the business. Members of management made explicit the values relating to the employment of people, the crucial ingredient of business success, and also worked through the implications of these in terms of how people were to be used, developed, rewarded, managed and so on. Such thinking has an 'open systems' emphasis; that is, it starts from the premise that an organization is not necessarily constrained by the forces acting on it but rather it can exert influence on its various environments through conscious thought and action. It is thus able better to control its own destiny and take some of the uncertainties out of forward planning.

The writer was involved in a similar exercise within BOC and an extract from the original 1973 version of the BOC Gases Division's Statement of Management Philosophy is attached in the first Appendix to the paper. It consisted of an overall statement of business philosophy, key objectives, their implications both technical and social for the various parts of the business, background thinking and a section on implementation. This proved to be the springboard for many progressive personnel developments within the division and was triggered jointly by the business planning process and by a widespread data collection of people's concerns, which indicated the need for a fundamental re-appraisal of management style.

Once the 'people values' and their implications have been worked through, it is much easier not only to define the personnel roles but, even more important, to have them recognized as key contributions to business success. There is also a much wider recognition of the support nature of the personnel contribution, that managers have a responsibility for the growth and development of their own people, for their effective use, which they cannot delegate. But managers can expect to call on a great deal of help from the personnel function. A copy of a recently developed statement of personnel roles in Babcock Power and Process Engineering Group is included in Appendix 2 on page 39 which illustrates this point.

Apart from prompting the debate around values and their implications for how the business is run, the senior personnel manager has still much to do before the changes become fully established. He or she needs to act as a conscience every time actions are planned by management which deviate from, or undermine belief in, management's commitment to practising the kind of management style made explicit in the *Statement of Management Philosophy*. He also has a major task on his hands in helping his personnel staff to appreciate the significance of the newly defined roles for them individually and particularly the change of emphasis from maintaining to developing; from 'doing for' to 'supporting in the doing of'; from doing that which is requested to confronting management sometimes with whether this is the right way; from dealing with problems as they arise to diagnosing and anticipating them and often having to help managers face unpleasant realities, so that necessary actions can be taken.

This change in approach can be very threatening to well established personnel people and, almost invariably, they will need help through training and support to develop the necessary self-confidence. Some may not have the necessary tolerance of uncertainty to do other than stay in the more administrative roles which continue to be important. Provided that they are not the arbiters of whether systems change or not, this is unlikely to present any difficulties but to leave them operating in the more progressive, problem-focused areas would be to give this aspect of personnel work the 'kiss of death'.

KEY EMPHASES IN THE DEVELOPING PERSONNEL ROLE

Much of what appears in this section will have been touched on before but I should like to draw together and develop some of the new emphases which one would expect to be apparent in a personnel function with a 'change focus' to its work.

1 A business orientation

A business orientation is critical because it provides a focus and integration for the many personnel contributions and does much to avoid the fragmentation trap already mentioned. It not only encourages the development of roles which have a business significance but, and this is vital, it requires personnel people to keep themselves fully informed of the developing business goals and changing business environment.

There is another important implication if a good personnel contribution is important to business success, personnel managers at all levels should be members of their local management teams by right. In this way the people aspects of the business can be seen to be of equal importance to the economic and technical and a full and effective contribution can be made. At the top of the organization the personnel manager should report to the managing director. If he or she reports through someone he is insulated from the wide-ranging view which is important to his full contribution, and the independent viewpoint which he should be able to give and which his managing director needs is compromised.

2 A diagnostic approach

Such an approach is concerned with both anticipating and avoiding problems and also with identifying areas where human energy is being wasted and where changes are necessary to improve organizational effectiveness. It is a key part of a pro-active personnel contribution. The personnel officer is in a uniquely good position to diagnose the frustrations and alienations symptomatic of human energy waste. He or she is the person to whom people speak when they are frustrated or upset. Rather than just providing a shoulder to cry on and then sending the individual away feeling better for having unburdened himself, he should check whether other people are feeling the same way. He is in a unique position for spotting incipient problems. All personnel officers should be capable of this kind of diagnosis, of probing to find whether problems are to do with style, unclear or conflicting objectives, structural deficiencies, unclear roles, inadequate systems or bad work organization.

3 A change planning/implementation facility

This goes much beyond the diagnostic stage mentioned in the previous section. It is having the ability to plan the kinds of changes which are necessary, to determine the sequence of change actions and levels of intervention which are likely to give a successful change strategy, and also having an awareness of the dynamics of change: for example, how to get management to face the problems and recognize the need for change action and how to involve those who will be affected so that, in the end, there is commitment to them and not opposition or sabotage.

This kind of role, as already mentioned, puts great demands on the individual. He needs to have developed sufficient credibility and to have sufficient self confidence to confront realities which managers would rather avoid and to challenge courses of actions which could have disastrous consequences. He must be able to tolerate uncertainty and take personal risks otherwise he cannot make a meaningful contribution.

There is no way in which one could expect every personnel type to have, or indeed develop, these highly sophisticated OD skills but there is a need in every organization for this kind of resource. Whether it should be based in personnel is open to debate. If it is not, the danger is that the OD man is forever seen as rocking the personnel boat, suggesting this or that change. If, on the other hand, the activity is part of the personnel function's work it can sharpen the department's focus on change and there is a much greater likelihood that the need for appropriate changes within the personnel systems will be recognized. Although, the activity then loses some of its independent third party quality, the writer believes that this is the preferred base.

4 Concern with the 'hows' of the business 'whats'

In general, management is much better at deciding what should be done than at deciding how decisions should be implemented. The 'hows' are usually assumed or, at the best, given limited time for debate. This is an area where the personnel member of the management team should play a major part. He should develop the ability to think through the behavioural implications of implementing decisions in the ways suggested and, where these are negative, be able to suggest alternative courses for achieving the same ends with much more positive effects.

33

Using a formula which the writer developed some time ago,

$$\text{decision} + \text{commitment} = \text{implementation},$$

the personnel man should always be advising on the ways to gain commitment to decisions.

5 *Sense of team and integrated effort*

It is desirable that the various sub-divisions of personnel report to one manager or director. This allied to a business focus, helps to avoid fragmentation. But this is not the whole story. Concentration within each sub-division on its own particular contribution/expertise can still lead to a lack of unity. An integrated effort will only take place when it is consciously fostered, when 'people problems' are looked at in a comprehensive way and total solutions sought which might well make an impact on the work and approach of several of the sub-divisions. This is perhaps the hardest task of all for the manager and the necessary integration can only come if he fosters a real sense of team spirit and devotes time to team-building activities.

6 *New skills*

Even if organization development work is not part of the personnel responsibility, the following skills will be required in some measure. If it is an intrinsic part, they will be required to a very high level of competence indeed.

(a) *Diagnostic*—the ability to get behind the symptoms to the real root causes of problems. Sometimes it will be necessary to recognize that personnel people are not the ones to deal with these causes. Other experts (eg method study, planning, systems engineering, etc) will often be required. Sometimes multi-disciplinary effort will be desirable.

(b) *Behavourial*—structures and systems have a direct impact on the way people behave. Conflicts are often caused by inadequacies in structures and systems. Changes in these are then much more appropriate than team-building activities which are aimed at helping people to work together better. In such instances improving inter-personal competence can do no more than deal with the symptoms of the basic problems.

An ability to predict the behavourial effects of various structures and systems is therefore important but sometimes there will be inter-personal and inter-group difficulties which are not caused by structural inadequacies, their resolution will then necessitate considerable inter-personal skills.

(c) *Organization design*—there is now a whole body of well-validated theory on the design of organizations, how to structure to effect various tasks, how the degree of environmental uncertainty affects structure, how different functions need to be organized differently to meet the organization's goals and how, with widely differentiated structures, integrating mechanisms and roles become crucially important. As these issues have a profound impact on the effective use or otherwise of people in organizations, the personnel function should maintain an expertise in this important area.

(d) *Role clarification*—a great deal of human energy can be wasted because of lack of clarity. The overall objectives may be clear and the structures right but the process is seldom carried on down the line to the point where the individual understands his contribution relative to those of his colleagues and his boss and how it fits into the overall effort. Personnel people should be able to help people develop meaningful job descriptions and a great deal of the management by objectives thinking is of value here and, in particular, team approaches to job definition.

(e) *Team building*—skills in reducing conflict have already been mentioned but these can be taken much further. Because of the complexity and differentiation of our organization structures, there is always the danger of parochial attitudes developing. Team building efforts as a means of helping to highlight and manage the interdependence of units in achieving a better overall result, is a key area of skill requirement.

PROBLEMS WHICH ARE LIKELY TO BE ENCOUNTERED IN DEVELOPING A MORE PROGRESSIVE PERSONNEL ROLE

Though the prize of an organization which makes the best use of its human potential, and a personnel function which is playing a leading and dynamic part in making it happen, is well worth striving for, it would be foolish to imagine that the transformation can be effected overnight or without considerable difficulty and many setbacks.

Credibility has to be earned in the new roles, in particular the ability to influence without executive authority, and this can only be achieved after positive results have been demonstrated. The first problem is how to get in, how to persuade managers to let personnel people experiment with new kinds of help. This is a slow process and highly dependent upon the calibre of the people taking part. Some will not have the necessary disposition and skills and others will actively oppose the proposed changes. In running and developing their systems many will have generated a considerable amount of personal power to say how things should be done. In industrial relations, for example, this power often verges on the executive. The industrial relation manager is like the spider at the centre of a complex web which he has painstakingly constructed. His access to information and ability to influence are widespread and it is a brave manager indeed who risks rocking the boat against the advice of his expert.

What has such a person to gain from change other than a loss of influence and the prospect of putting in a considerable amount of effort in order to develop and learn how to play a new game with new rules. Strangely, such highly respected and highly dedicated people can be the most powerful blocks to the kinds of change which have been described. Fundamental change is the last thing they want.

Another problem likely to be encountered is the obverse of the one just described. For the younger staff with names to make, there is much more visibility and kudos in being involved in the developmental side of personnel work. The danger with them is that they can all too easily go overboard on it and neglect the more mundane but very necessary administrative side of their jobs, and thus give the function a reputation for inefficiency or lack of urgency.

Of all the problems in developing a personnel function of the kind described, perhaps the main one is in trying to rush the changes. The writer has not avoided the trap and has recognized how important it is to make progress slowly. A time span of three to four years should be considered normal for reorienting a personnel function.

CONCLUSION

An attempt has been made to outline the kind of personnel contribution which is pertinent to the changing world in which we live. It has covered key aspects of new contributions, an approach which might be adopted to legitimize the developing role and some of the problems which might be encountered. It is hoped that the reader will be able to avoid some of the pitfalls by learning from the writers experience. Whatever the setbacks which might be encountered, it is considered unlikely that once started he will ever wish to turn back.

APPENDIX 1   BOC—GASES DIVISION

STATEMENT OF MANAGEMENT PHILOSOPHY

1   *Business philosophy*

In its core gases business, from a position of continuing dominance of the UK and Irish industrial and medical gas markets, the Division is concerned to maximize its contribution to the long-term profitability of the BOC Group through the most effective use of its resources, ie people, money and materials.

In its other businesses, ie Gas Services, Special Gases and Offshore Services, the Division's objective is primarily one of growth, development and diversification with medium rather than short-term profit the primary consideration.

2 *Key overall objectives*

To identify and realise profitable market opportunities for expanding and diversifying the Division's range of activities.

To improve the leadership and management of the people employed and to create conditions whereby employees at all levels are encouraged, and enabled, to use and develop their potentials and are therefore motivated to make an increasing contribution towards the achievement of Divisional and Group objectives.

To provide the BOC Group with management talent and with ideas capable of profitable development.

To carry out all its operations in such a way as to safeguard the health, safety and environment of its employees and the public.

3 *Implications for management philosophy*

In running its business, Divisional Management is faced with managing both a social system of people and their organization and the technical system of physical equipment and resources. The optimization of its overall operations can only be achieved through the joint optimization of the two systems. Attempts to optimize the two independently of each other or to place undue emphasis on one or the other can only lead to an overall operation which is less than optimally effective. (An analysis of the 'technical' and 'social' implications of the various parts of the business was also included here.)

4 *Background thinking*

Most of the implications for the various social systems are concerned with the development of the Division's employees.

We recognize that we cannot expect them to become committed to the necessary changes in response to mere exhortation. We must set out to create conditions under which such changes will be possible. It will be necessary to go beyond providing satisfactory terms and conditions of service, important though these are. We shall have to help each individual meet some of his deeper needs from his job:

to have a content which is reasonably demanding in terms other than sheer endurance and to have variety

to know what the scope of the job is and how well he is performing it

to have the opportunity for personal growth and possibly advancement

to have some discretion in decision-taking

to have appropriate social support and recognition

to be able to relate what he is doing to the wider business.

Though most men have these needs their relative significance varies from individual to individual and differing jobs provide opportunities for going some way towards meeting individual needs.

However, as tasks almost invariably involve other people, we cannot look at jobs in isolation. In developing organizational forms we must observe certain principles:

the individual must know not only what he is required to do but also the ways in which his work ties in with what others are doing

he must know what part he plays in the communications network

he must know the limits within which he has genuine discretionary powers

he must know clearly what objectives he is aiming to achieve

though managers should ensure that responsibility and authority go hand-in-hand to avoid people being delegated responsibility without having the means to exercise it, we want people to take initiatives and not accept constraints without challenge

managers must be prepared to increase the responsibility of their subordinates when capabilities are unused

managers must be prepared to accept the risks attendant on greater delegation in the belief that they will be greatly outweighed by the benefits

the Division must seek to ensure that status and reward are consistent with contribution

there must be greater openness in the information made available at all levels

we must ask ourselves 'what are we obliged to withhold' rather than 'what are we obliged to say'

we must identify peoples' ideas, frustrations and constraints and use them as a basis for stimulating appropriate changes.

5   Implementation of the philosophy

The most effective achievement of our business results will only be possible if our action plans, structures, working relationships etc manifest the spirit of the philosophy. Verbal or written communications alone will not be sufficient; it is essential that all employees be enabled to relate the philosophy to themselves by participating in its implementation in their own parts of the division.

A special burden or responsibility rests with the senior managers. Starting with their commitment, it will be possible to involve progressively the other levels of employees in searching out the implications for themselves.

APPENDIX 2 BABCOCK POWER & PROCESS ENGINEERING GROUP—ROLE OF THE PERSONNEL FUNCTION

OVERALL ROLE

To provide the basic personnel service and the skills necessary to support line management in achieving the Group's business objectives through the most effective and just use of its employees. To this end to help develop the climate which leads to a highly motivated and committed workforce and the full use and development of the potential of all members of the organization.

SPECIFIC ROLES

1 *Organization change and development*
To maintain an awareness of changes in the Group's business objectives and of changes in its environment so as to help management:

anticipate and prevent the development of problems in the Group's human systems
identify and solve existing problems
plan organization changes.in such a way as to gain the commitment and support of employees and a better achievement of the Group's goals

2 *Manpower planning*
To help senior management develop the forward manpower plans for making available the numbers of people, skill and experience necessary to the achievement of its long-term aims and to maintain balanced age distributions.

3 *Succession and career planning*
To produce and run the system, provide the data etc. necessary for management to carry out effective succession, management development and more general staff development planning and the transfers necessary to make them possible.

Within this to produce and administer an effective performance appraisal programme.

4 *Training/development*
With management, to identify the training needs emerging from 2 and 3 and then either to provide it internally or arrange for it to be provided externally.

To identify with management where on-the-job development is more appropriate than training.

5 Rewards systems

To develop and maintain rewards structures which lead to the maintenance of proper differentials, which are flexible and yet perceived as fair, which are properly related to the market place and which support the behavourial patterns necessary to the achievement of the Group's business objectives.

6 Recruitment and selection

To assist line management in the recruitment of staff by selecting the optimum means of recruitment and by providing the necessary screening, joint interviewing and administrative support.

7 Separation, redundancy and early retirement

To generate policies and approaches for encouraging early retirement, for dealing constructively with redundancy problems whenever such action becomes necessary, and for dealing with medical retirements.

To contribute to Babcock & Wilcox Limited's thinking in this area.

8 Employee relations
(a) Hourly paid

To take intiatives in developing creative working relationships with the trades unions such that:

(i) changes necessary to the achievement of desired business results can take place without disruption of the Division's operations

(ii) Better utilization and flexible use of employees is achieved in return for more responsible and more satisfying jobs and better pay conditions of service and pay

(b) Staff

(i) To help develop the climate and management style in which staff are able to put forward ideas for change and raise both legitimate concerns and ideas for constructive change in the knowledge that they will be dealt with in a positive way.

(ii) To ensure that terms, conditions and levels of reward are such that these are not the prime motivations for staff unionization

If the desire for unionization grows, as seems likely, to ensure, in so far as possible, that the developments lead to a situation of co-ordinated staff representation rather than inter-union rivalry and leap-frogging

(c) All employees represented by unions

(i) To support line management in dealing with complaints and disputes raised by unions within the agreed disputes procedures

(ii) To stimulate the development of progressive industrial relations policies

(iii) To contribute to periodic negotiations with the unions on wages/salaries and general conditions of employment

9 *Employment legislation*
To have a full understanding of legislation impacting directly on employees in terms of their employment, conditions and involvement, to interpret and advise management on these matters, to develop policies reflecting the requirements of employee legislation and to monitor that we are operating within the law.

10 *Administration and records*
To administer the Company's various welfare and other personnel services.

To maintain such personnel records as are necessary for the organization and to meet the need for information, both statutory and by Babcock & Wilcox Ltd.

11 *Personal counselling*
To provide counselling and personal support to any of the Group's employees who require help or wish to share a problem.

12 *Development of the personnel role*
To seek continually to improve the effectiveness of the personnel contributions in support of the Group's business activities.

CHAPTER III

The introduction of OD to the organization

Arthur Chapman

One of the questions most commonly asked about OD concerns how it may be introduced to an organization. Arthur Chapman, a personnel specialist of many years experience, describes with examples the way OD was introduced in two organizations. He stresses the point that there is no one way of introducing OD and, even more importantly, he argues that once OD is introduced this should not be regarded as its first and last beginning. Initiating OD should be seen as a continuous process.

The problems associated with the entry of OD to organizations are also discussed and the author offers some suggestions for dealing with them.

The title of this chapter appears to suggest that the beginning of OD activity in an organization is a particular, once and for all event. In fact there may be many beginnings and these are not all simply 'false starts' (although there may be those too!). If you were to ask people working in different parts (levels and functions) of any organization when and where OD started, you would be likely to get different answers. In my own company some managers might see the starting point as some years ago when they first began to get interested in understanding the human side of organization. Others would identify the beginning of OD with the decision to work with a particular consultant. Many would probably see a residential course they attended as the beginning. There would also be some who would respond to the question by asking, 'What OD?' Thus describing the commencement of OD is not so straightforward as it might at first appear.

This chapter will deal with introducing OD to the organization in the following sequence:

the concept of readiness for change in an organization
matching the OD approach and the organization

how to start
advantages and disadvantages of personnel sponsorship
OD as a main line management activity
many beginnings

THE CONCEPT OF READINESS FOR CHANGE IN AN ORGANIZATION

The current environment provides plenty of opportunity for organizations to begin OD work. Their chief executives and personnel departments are bombarded with invitations to accept help from this consultant or that institution. However, making a real start depends not so much on the availability of advice from outside as on the state of readiness of the organization itself. The first general point to be made is that, for OD to make a healthy beginning, it has to be a response to a need felt within the organization. It is unlikely to be felt even by all the *managers* at the outset but there has to be a 'critical mass' to engender the birth of the process. It is probably true that the more senior the managers who conceive the idea of a planned change process, the smaller in numbers may be this critical mass. In my own organization, the considerable impetus of the OD project from the start was undoubtedly because the stimulus came from a group of senior managers including the chairman and the managing director.

A general interest in 'people type' activities is not sufficient. There must be substantial support for the need to make enquiries about the state of the organization, about its goals and its processes. These questions may be primarily related to the past. For example, people in the organization may feel that the changes time has wrought may be more loss than gain or that there is not so much involvement and commitment as in the past. Such questions may also relate to the present. For instance, where is the organization going? or why are there inter-departmental difficulties? or why is communication so much more of a problem than previously? Questions like these may be no more than the expression of an aimless nostalgia. If so, they may not be real or significant enough to stimulate action.

The source of the concern to review may also come from outside. This may stem from competition in the market place or from a realization that the organization is being left behind in technology and innovation. New values and expectations in society may be experienced as pressure for change. Also stimuli for change may come because people are aware of the need to 'change with the times' or because they have ideals to which they wish to give expression. Employees may feel a want to have a hand in making the future. They may not be satisfied to sit back and wait for it in the hope that the organization will cope. A sort of tension may grow in an organization because the past seems to have been brighter than the present or because people can envisage a better future. Perhaps the organization does not meet the challenge of its environment as it should—or must if it is to survive. Or maybe there is an inbalance within the organization between commercial activities, technology and the way in which people are dealt with and used. Whether this tension is sufficient to lead to the start of a change programme is at least partly a matter of who feels the tension and who is asking the questions. One way or another there must be enough *will* for change if anything is to happen.

I can compare two companies in their readiness for change of this sort. One was the British subsidiary of a large multinational company; the other, a medium sized consumer goods manufacturer. Both of them, in different ways, had had a long term interest in progressive employment policies. The multinational company had for example employed one of the pioneers of the management training approach to OD, Ralph Coverdale. He eventually set up his own consultancy long before OD had any widespread appeal in this country. The management training course he had developed continued to be used in the company and was attended over a period of years by almost every manager and supervisor in mixed level and function groups. In some cases, usually where the entire management teams were trained over a short time, the change process affected methods of groups working and there was some real development of that part of the organization.

My own involvement began when I was appointed head of the development and training department in the personnel function in the London head office. It seemed to me that there was a *prima facie* need for a deeper and wider process to help people in the organization to be clearer about its role and goals as a subsidiary of a foreign company; and also to relate the new management style beginning to be established here and there to the company's role and goals. So I did a 'market survey' of the range of OD approaches then available. The variety on offer made it possible to look for a match between the characteristics of the company and those of the OD programme. The attempt to arouse interest in a possible OD project proved to be a fruitless and frustrating experience. It seemed to be impossible to carry top management along to the point of recognizing any connection between the company's needs and what organization development had to offer. I had to face the possibility that what was lacking was perception and skill on my part. With the benefit of long hindsight, it seems that a much more significant cause was the lack of any will for change in an organization which felt no real responsibility for its own future. Not only were board members constantly looking over their shoulder for reactions from their US parent but also even specialist departments like personnel were tightly controlled in the objectives they pursued and in the methods they used.

In contrast, the other company enjoyed complete independence. Even the principal shareholders were active in the management of the business and they were not a separate force to be deferred to. It was also a family business in which the paternalism of an earlier generation had been succeeded by a much more informed interest in behavioural science. But at the time when I joined the company, the interest was somewhat academic. Although there was a strong current of humanitarianism, work on personnel philosophy and management style were not seen by most managers to have much to do with the overall health and vitality of the organization. Nevertheless, there was some interest at the top and questions were being asked by directors, especially by the chairman and the managing director, about the meaning and relevance of OD. One of the first pieces of paper put before me when I joined the company as personnel director asked for advice about the most suitable OD approach for the company's needs.

As part of my survey of OD approaches, I had encountered a particular consultancy organization and a renewed contact with them reminded me of their experience *inter alia* with family businesses. I arranged a meeting between our chairman and the consultant's UK representative, which was followed by a top management seminar. We agreed that this would be the basis on which we and the consultant would decide whether we wished to work together. We eventually decided that we could collaborate and that seminar was the start of a long lasting and fruitful partnership.

The contrast between my experience of trying to introduce OD in those two companies could hardly have been greater and it was all the more pointed because the second experience followed so hard upon the heels of the first. Undoubtedly there was an element of chance in all this but, looking back, the real difference undoubtedly seems to have been in the states of readiness of the two organizations.

MATCHING THE OD APPROACH AND THE ORGANIZATION

At the time of my unsuccessful attempt to interest top management in the large multinational in OD, I had judged the above consultant's approach to be somehow inappropriate to that organization, without quite understanding why. In the light of later experience I came to see that my underlying assumption was the concept of a match between a particular OD approach and a specific company. The consultant's approach was congruous with the smaller company, according to this assumption, because there was a match. The organization had recently emerged from a characteristic pioneer phase and there were (and still are) many residual signs of the personal note in relationships with employees and customers. The consultancy in question for its part builds its work on a concept of man which sets a high value on individuals, their ideals, feelings and thinking The multinational on the other hand, was in a different phase of development.

Functions were highly specialized and differentiated. Personal concern and warmth were not particularly valued. Professionalism was all. At the time, I felt that something like Reddin's 3-D[43] approach fitted that company well. The diagnosis of management style in terms of task and relationship orientation connected with earlier work and the addition of the third dimension of effectiveness as a means of relating orientation to the needs of the situation seemed highly appropriate.

As we have seen, finding a satisfactory match is not a sufficient condition for progress but it is probably a necessary one. The cynic might also point out that accident and luck seem to have something to do with success here as elsewhere. Looking back, it certainly seems to me that chance played a part in both the failure and success recounted above. It may be a spurious candour to describe as good fortune what some would call opportunism. Nevertheless, the start of the successful OD process in the second example was masked by some happy accidents, for example, the good fortune that an unplanned second contact with the particular consultant coincided with a question within the organization about OD and that the chairman of the company and the consultant appeared to hit it off together from the start. At the time the match between company and consultant was not so clear as it became later. In any case determining such a match would have been difficult for someone who had joined the company so recently. So there may well have been an element of accident in that too. But whether by accident or design, one component of a satisfactory match between a company and an OD approach which is probably vital is in their values and philosophy. Companies, like individuals, have their values and their assumptions. And it may be that what is most important in making the match is congruence of underlying beliefs and values. The hypothesis that suggests itself is that, to be successful in bringing about the radical and necessarily long-term changes which constitute a genuine development of the organization, an OD approach needs a strong, coherent and consistent set of values.

How to start

It has been contended earlier in this chapter that a prerequisite of organization development is that there are significant, live questions about goals and practices within the enterprise. These furnish an essential will for change which can overcome the organization's inertia. So the first stage in a strategy of change may be to explore questions which are extant; to test the will for change; and to attempt to define a long range picture of the future. A process in some ways like this marked the beginning of the OD work in my present company, when our top management group produced their picture of the future for the company. Beckhard maintains that it is better to start by defining today's problems than tomorrow's hopes, on the ground that working on the picture of the future may distort the view of issues in the present. He has a point and wishful thinking may underestimate the difficulty of current problems. That is the price tag on that approach. Nevertheless, doing it the other way round, that is by diagnosing present ills, also carries a penalty for the size and complexity of those ills may inhibit action. There may just not be enough will to improve. No doubt both approaches are suited to different situations. Both methods can lead quickly to the identification of specific tasks. In our case, it took six months to move from a group of senior managers' clarifying their picture of the future to a stage when a wider group identified some pressing, current problems as development issues. Arguably, to have begun with a probing of present difficulties might have enabled us to begin to focus on those issues sooner. In fact, most of the 'delay' was needed to allow the consultant to familiarize himself with the company and was therefore probably inevitable.

Both of these strategies are characterized by an early identification of pressing issues which need urgent attention and can also serve as vehicles for learning about development. This means that a relatively small number of managers in specific parts of the organization become involved in OD activities and begin to gain some insights into the nature of development. (The 'reciprocal', of course, is that the majority is not involved at all). Given reasonable and evident success, a degree of confidence in the value of OD is established at least with some managers. In our case this provided a springboard to a management training activity across a much broader front, in which all managers and supervisors went through an 'unfreezing' course in 'diagonal slices'—mixing levels and functions. Some strategies begin with the unfreezing effect of a course for many managers. The Coverdale courses in my earlier experience in the multinational company *could* have been such a stage, but they were not seen to be such at the outset and so were seldom followed up effectively.

The traditional organization change process has been one of restructuring. Often the new allocation of duties and the new organization chart were a substitute for, not an expression of, change. I have no direct experience of beginning an organization development project with a restructuring exercise and my feelings about restructuring after four years of OD work are that it seems to follow on naturally from action on the content and process of work rather than precede it. But I can envisage situations where a new structure, for example a new site or a new department, provides great potential for effective development work. Any situation where people are formed into new groups offers such an opportunity. One might go further with this line of thinking. For example, when an organization has been consciously developing itself for some time, the range of issues which can be seen and dealt with as development issues widens considerably. It becomes difficult to see problems which do *not* have potential to

47

provide learning for individuals or groups. The question then is whether there are enough people around the company who can extract the development value from such problems. The whole effort will be much more likely to suceed if, from the beginning of OD work, people in different parts of the organization are trained as resources. One way we have found to be effective is to use line managers, not just consultants and personnel specialists, as trainers on the training course mentioned above. Teaching and practising new concepts brings a high level of commitment and provides a widely dispersed resource.

ADVANTAGES AND DISADVANTAGES OF PERSONNEL SPONSORSHIP

The personnel department is most likely to be the vestibule through which OD enters an organization. Personnel people are likely to be attracted to concepts of development with a strong emphasis on team and individual development. They may also see OD as a route to greater influence and be tempted to foster a sense of the elusive mystery beyond the veil through their effortless command of the jargon, 'client systems', 'interventions', 'change agent' and the rest. But, less cynically, behavioural science jargon is not invented by them and they may be the best available bridge between the behavioural science theorist and the managerial practitioner.

The reason why OD may have an attraction as the way to power and influence is that many personnel departments lack, and would like to have, such influence in their companies. And that is why there is a strong case against personnel sponsorship, not that it would necessarily be a bad thing if they had more influence. But unfortunately, in many organizations, they are miles away from the centre of things even though they may be closer than ever before. For many managers the essential contribution of the personnel department is seen as a servicing of the people element in the enterprise. The function exists to keep the vagaries and embarrassments of human beings away from line managers, thus enabling them to attend to the 'real' tasks of the organization. Thus the problem is that, if OD comes in through the personnel department, it may be irretrievably labelled a 'people thing' and may not stand a chance of demonstrating what it has to offer as a means of synthesis for the commercial, technological and social components in the company. Of course, in an increasing number of organizations, the personnel function has a central and, not a peripheral role in the life of the company; in others it may be commissioned to introduce OD by a chief executive or a board who are concerned about developing the organization.

There is the possibility that an interested top management may decide to put someone outside the personnel function in charge of OD work. In the only case of this approach I have met, OD did seem to escape the 'people thing' label, at least in the initial phase—but at the cost of the alienation and hostility of the personnel department.

Commonly, many of the difficulties of introducing OD are avoided by using an outside consultant. At least he starts off with the honour of a prophet from another country. He can remain independent of any particular function, but at the same time he can form direct relationships with all of them including personnel, who need not then feel excluded. He is also a convenient receptacle for complaint and frustration when 'growing pains' are felt!

Increasingly the initiative for change may come from managers in any function and at any level in the organization, as they are exposed in their early or late education to concepts of social change. They also share society's growing awareness of changing values about people and their work, and may see in some of the concepts of development ways of giving practical effect to these values. It would be healthy, in my view, if more pressure for OD work came not from personnel or from top management but from people in other parts of companies. To be effective, even such pressure would have to win the backing of top management if OD were to be taken into the system.

The question of values is an important one not only in matching a specific OD approach with a particular company. It is probably also important that whoever sponsors the work should have some values, goals or expectations in common with the organization. If the sponsor's philosophy is incompatible with the organization's, whether he is a consultant, someone from the personnel department or a specially appointed project manager, he will be rejected sooner or later. His frame of reference will be obscure and his objectives misunderstood or, if understood, unacceptable. Unfortunately at times personnel departments are almost expected to have values and goals which are different from, somehow vaguely higher than, those of the rest of the organization—as though the organization were reluctant to lose the last shreds of morality and vision but tidied them all away into the personnel cupboard.

OD AS A MAIN LINE MANAGEMENT ACTIVITY

The personnel function is likely to remain the natural channel for behavioural science knowledge in much the same way as theoretical work in university laboratories or industry research associations is mediated to companies through research and development departments. But personnel departments serve well the cause of developing their organizations when they encourage colleagues to see development possibilities in every situation and to see 'development' not simply in terms of developing people as individuals. For 'development' in the phrase 'organization development' ought to mean a process of consciously managed change in the total economic—cum-technological—cum-social system of the enterprise.

In this broad sense OD must be a main line management activity, not just a specialist activity. If it is anything more than an in and out, asset-stripping, get-rich-quick operation, management must share with OD a strong sense of time, constantly evaluating the past, observing and understanding the present and predicting and assessing possible futures. Management and OD both try to gain an insight into situations which goes beyond observation and seeks an understanding of processes. Seeing people as 'the most important asset in the business' is not just a well-worn phrase from company reports, it is a view shared by effective managers and OD.

The point of emphasizing the common viewpoint of managers and OD is that a real effort should be made to plant OD concepts and activities right in the main stream of the enterprise and not allow them to create just a few eddies in some sidestream. Usually this means enlisting line managers in such activities in every way possible. I have already mentioned their involvement as trainers in a company management training course (there were 10 of them, senior and middle managers, including four directors). They still constitute a highly committed group of people which provides a reinforcement to development work whether acting together as a group of trainers, or separately as managers who influence important segments of the company in their normal roles. Quite a number of the managers have also become involved. Some of them who were not trainers, after attending the course as participants, wished to become more closely associated with the development work and helped with counselling or in project work. Others joined the central steering committee or sat on one of the working parties guiding particular development projects. Amongst the activities initiated by these managers have been:

volunteering a major business expansion programme as an organization development project

creating many new opportunities for personal growth through job rotation and enrichment work in a factory

working in a constructive way with individuals whose roles do not seem to fit their abilities.

MANY BEGINNINGS

Only in a very superficial sense can the introduction of OD into the organization ever be said to be complete. At the beginning there is a recognition of starting something. But it is not development itself that is beginning but the consciousness of development and, with consciousness, the possibility of guiding the process. At that early stage making a beginning means finding a point of entry, choosing a time and an issue. Once the entry has been made, a process starts which affects only a part of the organization. As when climbing a range of hills, the conquest of one peak simply opens up the prospect of a still higher one. When we embarked on the major exercise of taking all our managers and supervisors through a course, we were already becoming aware that, important though that was in itself, there was a sense in which it merely prepared us for an even more challenging task, as we put it, 'to face the shop floor'.

As development work proceeds the perspective changes, there seem to be more challenges and opportunities. One becomes aware of the different needs of different levels of management and supervision or of the special requirements of particular departments. One looks again and sees development issues along the interfaces between departments. In one part of the organization a traditional culture, which seems to hold back people's development, provides a barrier to change. In another the opening of a new site offers the prospect of applying all the experience and learning available throughout the organization to a fresh situation.

Each one of these presents an entry problem, how to find a point of entry, an appropriate time, a suitable issue, a way of influencing a person with leverage. But entry too is a process about which much can be learned so that, with time, skill and insight are accumulated.

Many beginnings presuppose many continuings so maintenance as well as initiating processes have to be learned. Perhaps this is where the personnel function has a role in the developing organization which no one else can quite fill. It is almost an information function, recording not so much what has been done as what has been learned, recalling projects that are languishing and registering issues which need attention but are not yet 'ready'. It should be remembered that this has to be an unselfish role, having more to do with letting go and giving away than with holding on.

CHAPTER IV

The contribution of OD to the practice of personnel

A *Industrial relations*
B *Appraisal*
C *Training*
D *Job redesign*

A INDUSTRIAL RELATIONS

Mike Pedler and Malcolm Leary

In this highly challenging paper the authors show how the association of OD with 'truth and trust' is misplaced and suggest that OD has much to contribute in situations where 'conflict and power' feature strongly. With a framework for viewing industrial relations similar to that used in chapter 1 for describing development, they conclude that in industrial relations in the UK attention has been given mainly to regulation and control and little to integration, collaboration and adaptation. This is reflected in the narrow way conflict is seen, channelled and handled, and in the concern to protect the status quo. *The core of the developmental approach they outline is that it provides a set of ideas and values for a broader and deeper understanding of conflict (considering social as well as economic motives and needs). It also offers a range of methods for handling issues in different settings, evolving structure, behaviour and relationships together. Strategic options are viewed in the context of historical stages in unionization and industrial relations and these put some of the problems of formalization and over-concern for regulation into perspective.*

INTRODUCTION

Industrial relations has long been felt by many to be the core of personnel management practices and theory: the crossroads where the various interest groups involved in the organization meet, encounter, cooperate and inevitably sometimes conflict. As such, this aspect of organizational life is characterized by complexity and some confusion. There is little doubt, that the field of industrial relations is viewed as a key area when it comes to discussions regarding economic performance, better relationships or increased individual satisfaction.

Looking at the present industrial relations scene in Britain it is apparent that organization development has had very little impact on this field either in terms of perspective or technology. Management in some major companies such as ICI and Shell have shown continued interest and have even established OD functions. Even so examples of the successful application of development approaches to industrial relations are few and far between. There is some evidence perhaps of development thinking permeating through to certain areas of personnel practice, particularly training, but even here there is still much scepticism and opposition.

One reason for this indifference may be that industrial relations development is seen only as a peripheral activity with the more essential aspects being represented by 'power' struggles conducted between influential groupings. A recent survey of the 51 largest TUC affiliated unions concluded that:[44]

> trade unions know little of behavioural science methods or theory
> this is compounded by a general suspicion of and mistrust of anything new
> especially if it appears to emanate from management or their 'lackeys'
> behavioural science has yet to make any meaningful impact. Even those unions who were knowledgeable about behavioural science saw development activities being of marginal importance compared to what they considered to be key activities such as negotiation, representation and pressure grouping, 'it comes way after money and security—if these are wrong you can forget it'.

The general impression is that OD as an area of study is bracketed with the largely discredited 'human relations' school of management of the 1930s and '40s which has been more recently characterized as a 'unitary' frame of reference.[45]

The view of industrial relations from a development perspective is no less hostile or sceptical. Evidence from across the Atlantic supports the marginal image of OD *vis à vis* industrial relations. Development activities and experiments have largely flourished away from the hostile and barren areas of industrial relations.[46] The value systems and even practices of industrial relations and OD seem poles apart. OD practice is often caricatured as overflowing with 'love and trust' whereas industrial relations values are often seen as uncompromising and power based, with conflict being regarded as inevitable and immutable. Behind these caricatures, we see development perspectives and technology as having great value for industrial relations practice. There are undoubtedly many areas of joint concern.

53

The following sections of this paper will therefore consider:

the nature of industrial relations; its place and importance within society; its current dilemmas and needs; its processes and practices

organization development activities—particularly their shortcomings with regard to industrial relations systems and needs

an approach to industrial relations demonstrating the applications of development perspectives and technology.

THE NATURE OF INDUSTRIAL RELATIONS

Defining industrial relations is a celebrated activity amongst academics who specialize in the subject. Definitions proliferate from the narrowest 'institutionalist' viewpoint, through the 'rules and job regulations' focus, to the distribution of power and control arguments central to Marxist writers. More recently some sociologists have preferred the broad 'man in his working environment' stand point. Here we are more concerned with the practices of industrial relations, with attention on what people have to do, how they behave and relate to one another, and the processes within which they are engaged. More flexible and fluid views of industrial relations unfortunately tend to run counter to current academic orthodoxy. This orthodox approach tends to support the predominantly conservationist and static models.[47] Industrial relations is thus not generally conceived as something in process, continually and potentially dynamic. It is more usually seen as a precarious balance of interests which occasionally falls out of equilibrium. When this happens the balance must be quickly restored in order to maintain the *status quo*.

Britain is unusually and uniquely rich in the institutions, traditions and procedures of industrial relations. The individuals and groups concerned are often highly skilled at handling the current issues in their specialist field. We are therefore currently rich in analysis and diagnosis and our strength lies in understanding and using those processes concerned with containment, compromise and stability. We are perhaps weaker in understanding processes concerned with action, with change and movement. At the same time the traditional processes of industrial relations are being questioned on the basis of their ability to cope with present or future issues. The accepted boundaries between bargaining, consulting, participating, conflict handling and problem solving activities are becoming increasingly blurred in the face of internal and external pressures.

Mollander[48] has identified these pressures in terms of 'revolutions' of authority, information technology and education. There is general agreement on the basic responses which industrial relations systems have developed to deal with such influences:[49]

54

1 Regulation	— of aspects of production, employment and the distribution of power, wealth and rewards
2 Integration	— of individuals, groups and sections within a framework of law, custom and social norms
3 Participation and collaboration	— in decision making; managing conflicts; what goals should be attained and how? Who should be involved and at what level on which issues? Problems of both quality and extent of participation
4 Adaptation and revitalization	— responding appropriately to changes in values and authority; dealing with growth and decay.

There can be little doubt that the typical British system concentrates its energies upon the regulation function. A recent article, which summarizes contributions to the theory debate, concludes 'It is, however, now generally agreed that rules are the output of an industrial relations system . . .'[50] Since the report of the Donovan Commission[51] there has been what amounts to an obsession with formalization, codification and regulation of industrial relations behaviour. Whilst this is not necessarily a bad thing *per se*, it has led to a neglect of the other functions, especially the latter two. Integration is a function catered for by a traditional approach to industrial relations but only in a superficial way. The heavy accent upon rules ensures a high degree of compliance but scarcely guarantees commitment. Commitment is the result of highly integrated relationships which, at present, require a considerable extension of participation and shared decision making to bring them about. As an example we can take the fact that in 1976 strike figures in Britain were at their lowest for many years. Many commentators assumed from this observation that industrial relations were much 'better' than for some time. If 'better' means less overt conflict, then certainly there seems to be less open flouting of the rules. However, it is legitimate to ask if this implies that there is widespread commitment to the ends and goals of our industrial relations system? One counter-argument would be that absenteeism, 'sickness,' psychosomatic illness, poor timekeeping, 'daydreaming', general withdrawal of enthusiasm and lack of commitment at an individual level have replaced more traditional forms of industrial action as a way of attacking a system which has become much more adept at containing collective action. It might further be argued that this sort of individual withdrawal of effort, when aggregated, far outweighs the losses of industrial effort caused by collective action.

Concentration upon rules has not produced enough integration to ensure commitment, nor has it addressed itself to the other two functions of industrial relations systems, participation and collaboration and adaptation and revitalization.

Trade unions are in general only just beginning to think about the implications of participation and their uncertainties and divisions are only too obvious. Those managements which are now looking at participation are exploring the outlines of an emerging field, most of which is unexplored territory. The problems of decay in industrial relations systems and the need for continuous adaptation and revitalization have been the subject of even less thought and effort. For example, payment systems and job evaluation systems are known to have a fairly definite 'life' and are subject to decay. One has only to compare the amount of energy which goes into propping up decaying systems with that degree of effort used to plan for change to see how industrial relations systems (as of present conceived) favour fire-fighting and the *status quo* over any attempts at planned change.

There is apparently a need for a more dynamic, future-oriented view of industrial relations. Also we shall require a philosophy for generating appropriate ideas, concepts and values and a technology for translating these ideas into reality.

THE POTENTIAL OF A DEVELOPMENT APPROACH

A development approach would claim to be able to add such a dimension without ignoring the harder, conflictual aspects in the process.

In many cases a development perspective will in fact be used to highlight the dilemmas and clashes between what would appear on the surface to be irreconcilable positions, (for example between conflict and cooperation or between individual freedom and collective responsibility). We would further argue that in practice many of these central problems are forced underground by excessive channelling through formal procedures and institutionalization, only to surface again as other manifestations. In helping conflict to surface in all its forms, by assisting those concerned to understand its multifarious nature and to work towards better ways of overcoming, coping or learning to live with conflicts and confusions, a development approach has the potential to make a telling contribution. This potential has not been easy to realize in the hostile environment of industrial relations. There still remains a considerable gap between the theory and its practical application and between strategies and the practicable means needed to bring about action and a planned path of development.

THE BASIS OF A DEVELOPMENT APPROACH

We will use six specific areas to illustrate how such a development approach could operate in practice. By working on some of the most fundamental issues and dilemmas which industrial relations practice currently highlights we can begin to see what the addition of a developmental dimension might mean.

A TRADITIONAL INDUSTRIAL
RELATIONS VIEW IS

A DEVELOPMENT APPROACH TO
INDUSTRIAL RELATIONS CAN ADD

1 *Short-term oriented* ──────────────→ *a dynamic past and future view*

The structure of industrial relations in Britain has grown like Topsy from a long and distinguished industrial history. Its characteristics are, as we have seen, a voluntary, pragmatic view of life which results in a 'live for the day' mentality. The problems of the moment are for the most part so complex, the equilibrium to be maintained between many opposing forces so delicate that any suggestion of the introduction of a more forward looking, strategic concept is out of the question. Current industrial relations practice is firmly rooted in the past but only in relation to a rather narrow industrial and perhaps socio-political dimension. The present is concerned with maintenance activities, preserving the *status quo* if at all possible, and is essentially pessimistic in outlook. Expectations about longer term improvement, change and perhaps even a planned route of development are hard to find. However, a more healthy, optimistic view about possibilities can and does exist even within an essentially negative environment. This is especially so if the approach is firmly grounded on views of man and society which stress his essential nature in developmental rather than regressive terms.

2 *Economically myopic* ──────────────→ *a broader social dimension*

Industrial relations practitioners have perhaps tended in the past to over-emphasize the importance of economic factors. This is perhaps understandable given the industrial and economic basis of industrial relations activities. Without denying this essential economic bedrock, stress has more often been laid on the monetary and competitive elements within the economic sub-system than the more cooperative and inter-dependent factors which also undoubtedly exist alongside more visible manifestations. Changes to the system are only interpreted in narrow economic terms and only those developments which have an economic pay off really count. The broader social elements which also exist within the economic field tend to be ignored. Even when a social dimension is added this is done through legislative, macro channels and so the social organizational view of current activities is lost again. A more comprehensive approach to development would perhaps enable social questions within the organization to be raised and worked on for their own sake rather than be swamped within an excessively broad treatment of the problems or squeezed within narrow economic (monetary) constraints.

3 *Over-concerned with structures* ⟶ *options about behaviour as well as structure*

An exaggerated concern for rules, systems, procedures and institutions at the expense of behavioural elements involving roles and relationships has been supported by the underlying assumption that all problems can be sorted out by the right structural solutions. This emphasis on structures leads inevitably to a confrontation between those who wish to cling to existing frameworks and those who have a vested interest in radical change. The pious hope underlying both these positions is that if structures are changed the behaviour of those involved will adjust to meet new needs over a period. Even the evidence of rapid structural changes leaving behind generation-long behaviour adjustment problems (which can only be overcome in the short term by more rigid rules and repression) does not seem fundamentally to question this stance. In reality a complex interplay exists between structures and behaviour which must be understood and taken account of if lasting change is to be possible. A development approach offers a more evolutionary middle way towards structural change. This is more likely to take along with it those directly concerned, and at a pace that they can cope with.

4 *Reluctant to use outsiders* ⟶ *stress the value of a third party role*

Traditionally the third party role in industrial relations has been restricted to conciliation and arbitration. Serious problems of entry into established industrial relations systems are invariably encountered; this is evident even in situations where third party functions are institutionalized and written into agreements and procedures as an accepted process. There is a danger that the third party role, in order to become more acceptable, becomes restricted and formalized, thus locking itself into a series of inflexible, standardized stances and ways of working. A broader approach to questions of industrial relations development would see a much more creative and flexible role for the third party; this would mean helping the other parties concerned to clarify the different levels and types of conflict which are manifest as well as helping towards some resolution of the consequences. This would mean the outsider coming to understand the position of all other relevant parties from an independent standpoint, using a range of techniques and resources and generally acting as a catalyst.

5 *Concerned with bargaining* ⎯⎯⎯⎯⎯⎯⎯⎯⎯⎯⎯→ *a variety of techniques for resolving differences*

The major processes concerned with industrial relations activities are still bargaining and negotiating as a means of resolving differences, but this is far from the complete picture. It is too easy to see all industrial relations issues within organizations in terms of union/management conflict. On many occasions it would seem that, unless problems can be seen in this way, they are incapable of being handled adequately if at all.

Everything, it appears, must go through the negotiations 'sausage machine'. Many conflicts do not require negotiation in the formal sense, other techniques may be more appropriate to the circumstances. For example the following classification of issues looks at a variety of ways of resolving them:

information issues—using communication and conciliation methods
differences about means and methods—using communication and consultative approaches
clashes over goals and objectives—using negotiations and problem-solving
conflict over basic values and beliefs—work on the problem on an on-going basis rather than searching for an elusive 'solution'

A development approach may, as part of the overall process, aim to ventilate and even raise conflict into a form where it can be identified and dealt with. In fact this more sophisticated, open view of conflict is the core of a developmental approach.

6 *Concerned with conflict about goals* ⎯⎯⎯⎯⎯→ *views of conflict as being multi-faceted concerned with a variety of focuses and levels*

From a development point of view conflict is seen as having many possible causes and also many possible focuses, that is, points at which it clearly becomes seen and expressed. Consequently there are many possible resolution strategies. From an organizational standpoint, conflict can be conceived as occurring in a number of places and over a number of different issues.

The table on page 60 shows 16 possible types of conflict by placing issues against focuses in a simple matrix. The matrix has been kept deliberately simple to make the essential point that conflict is far from being a single-cause, single-focus phenomenon.

The focus of conflict affects choice of resolution strategy. Interpersonal conflicts require different approaches to intergroup ones. One could divide interpersonal conflicts into at least two major sub-types: boss-subordinate and peer conflict. Different approaches would be called for with each sub-type. Again there a

Conflict focus . . . Conflict Issue . . .	Inter-personal	Intra-group	Role	Inter-group
. . . Information				
. . . Means				
. . . Goals				X
. . . Values				

number of causes of conflicts within groups or within roles and role sets. For example, a role holder may be subjected to different and conflicting demands from one or more members of his role set, for instance, a foreman under pressure from both a shop steward and a production controller. Alternatively, the same foreman may get different messages from the same person at different times. For example, he may get demands both for 'production' and 'to keep the men happy' from his boss. Intergroup conflict can be management–union, but can equally be union–union, work group–work group (tool makers versus process workers) or quite frequently department–department (managers or teams are at loggerheads).

Because negotiation is the most legitimate form of conflict resolution under a traditional industrial relations system, conflicts tend to be expressed as *intergroup* (sub-type union–management) conflicts over *goals* (see matrix). Because the system is so well regulated all conflicts tend to be expressed in this way whatever their original level or focus. The different parties involved may bend or phrase them in this particular way simply to get them heard. As we have suggested earlier, there are many continuous conflicts in organizations which never do get heard at all but which nevertheless cost a great deal. Many of these conflicts are not 'real' conflicts, that is, problems of 'dissensus', they are frequently false conflicts or problems of lack of consensus.

Of course the above weaknesses of industrial relations cannot be applied to all situations and the claims made for a development dimension may be exaggerated in the face of certain barriers. Nevertheless we have perhaps established the basis of a more developmental approach to industrial relations which could be applied to a variety of organizational circumstances.

We shall now examine a wide range of organizational forms and indicate broadly how the addition of a development dimension might substantially alter the way in which the breadth and depth of strategies for improvement and change might be tackled.

DEVELOPMENT PHASES OF INDUSTRIAL RELATIONS

The nature and function of industrial relations in any organization is related to the stage of development of the system. Four stages of development are postulated:

1 unidentified
2 informal
3 formal
4 developing.

At the *unidentified* stage, an industrial relations situation exists but not in the consciousness of those involved, say managers and employees. In Britain today industrial relations is *unidentified* in many small concerns and in many areas of non-unionized employment. In the primary and manufacturing sectors these are often owner-managed, whilst in the service and professional sectors they abound in shops and offices of all descriptions. Pressure to change comes either from external pressures, such as changes in the law, or from the beginnings of collective activity by a part of the labour force.

The following key questions can indicate the existence of an *unidentified* industrial relations situation:

Has anyone in the organization any experience of industrial relations?
Does anyone in the organization have a formal responsibility for industrial relations?
Do you recognize industrial relations as an essential component in total business behaviour?
Have you considered how industrial relations can affect performance and efficiency as manifested in lack of productivity, absenteeism, lateness, low enthusiasm and morale, frequent sickness?
Are you aware of all requirements of legislation?
Are you complying with all legislative requirements?

Organizations which answer 'No' to all these questions could fairly be described as having an *unidentified* industrial relations situation. They will also want to ask themselves whether this is appropriate under their existing and prospective business conditions.

The second development stage is an *informal* industrial relations situation, where industrial relations is recognized as being important but where no formal procedures have been set up. The *informal* situation can develop from an

61

unidentified one, where external or internal pressures cause a feeling of 'discomfort' amongst senior management which eventually translates itself into action. Managerial action is always *ad hoc* and in response to pressure. Initiative is retained by management who use the *informal* nature of the system to their ends.

The following key questions can indicate the existence of an *informal* situation:

Do you have an industrial relations policy agreed at senior management or board level?

Are your employees formally represented?

Are your agreement and procedures written down?

Are managerial actions taken on the basis of planned policy rather than crisis responses to events?

Do you involve employees in decision making through systems of communication and consultation?

Do you have someone monitoring the effects of outside trends and pressures including legislation?

Organizations answering 'No' to these questions are likely to find increasing pressures building up to move towards a more formal situation at some time.

The *formal* situation is a response to internal or external pressures which have reached crisis point and where the situation is getting beyond the *ad hoc* control of the top management group. Increasing unionization among the labour force and a continual erosion via shopfloor bargaining of managerial prerogatives are possible internal pressures. The response is to establish formal, written procedures and agreements covering every area of union–management relationships; wage structures and differentials; collective bargaining machinery; and grievance, discipline, redundancy, communication and consultation procedures. Representation on the employee side is likely to be well defined, whilst designated members of management have specific industrial relations responsibilities. *Formal* situations are likely to be found wherever high density of unionization and large scale organization coincide. Hence it is found in most of Britain's large companies and is seen clearly in the nationalized industries and the public sector.

Key questions which can indicate the existence of a *formal* situation are:

Do you set up and operate:

(i) agreements at national and/or company level covering union recognition, wages and all terms of employment?

(ii) procedural rules covering industrial relations processes—communicating, consulting, disciplining, negotiating, problem solving?

(iii) systems and institutions to deal with specific matters such as representation, payment and differentials, redundancy, welfare, health and safety?

Do you provide and maintain adequate facilities for those involved in industrial relations to carry out their duties?

Developing industrial relations situations are by their very nature difficult to describe. Development of industrial relations will be borne out of a need to become more responsive and flexible and industrial relations patterns which emerge as a result will therefore take on more noticeable characteristics of fluidity and transience. Rather than describe an end state showing what a 'developed' industrial relations situation will look like we now examine some of the major characteristics which show themselves in *developing* industrial relations. For example, we envisage:

- a capacity for internal innovation and adaptation—from within the industrial relations system itself rather than imposed from outside
- a need to anticipate coming events as well as reacting to external circumstances
- the building up of an increased capability for innovation, foresight and initiative. As this capacity can only be developed within a broader social context this will involve strengthening the social aspects of industrial relations policy and planning
- the need to stimulate and assess initiatives and experiments
- alert and open management functions and processes
- more open and interdependent relationships across functions as well as within them.

In specific industrial relations terms it will certainly mean the creation of new institutions and media and the building up of new practices and skills. For those concerned it will mean taking on added responsibilities and roles and integrating these with the old. It will mean a sharing of responsibilities much more broadly than hitherto with a consequent need to live with the untidiness and uncertainty which this may cause along the way.

Already we have begun to indicate how the creation of a development approach to industrial relations might be started in certain areas. But we must, begin to identify the broad range of variables which need to be considered in determining an overall strategy.

A DEVELOPMENT STRATEGY FOR INDUSTRIAL RELATIONS

Development strategies by their very nature cannot be laid down for others to follow. They must emerge from consideration of what is needed by those whose commitment to the organization is involved. This means that all key individuals and groups within the organization need to be involved or given due consideration, either directly or through representatives. What follows are some guidelines to future practice in drawing up the bare bones of a development strategy for industrial relations. Already such an approach is being tried in some organizations or parts of organizations. To some extent the following notes form a distillation of existing good practice and conventional wisdom in this area. The following pointers to what might be appropriate may draw out a possible scenario for your organization to consider and debate. A development strategy for industrial relations will therefore need to contain:

1 A *future orientation*

Examination of future needs will demand a careful survey of the current climate and adequate discussion of the interpretation of this information. Alongside this activity working parties or study groups could perhaps be set up to draw out alternative views of what the future might look like. This will lead to more specific and deliberate joint planning on the type of industrial relations which *those concerned want to have*. The results of this planning exercise might be then used to formulate local social contracts or joint planning agreements.

This process will provide some experience which it will be hoped can generate optimism and confidence of joint control. This can be compared to the desperate, last ditch fire-fighting of traditional industrial relations which currently breeds pessimism, a sense of hopelessness and generates a mutual distrust and fear.

2 A *social development capacity*

In order to act as the powerhouse of ideas and questions on an essential social dimension to industrial relations developments, the capacity of the social sub-system will have to be built up. Again the first task may be of a diagnostic nature, building up information on such questions as:

What is the real commitment to social development which currently exists?
What are the real issues of social development which exists, that is, those which do not necessarily involve an economic motive?
What aspects of 'the organization-in-the-community' currently affect relationships?
What social developments are desired? Is there a real consensus on these issues?

This process may involve adopting methods which are not easily accepted by hard-nosed industrial relations practitioners who are used to other cultures.

Questions of social health and ecology, points underlying social contact factors are not easily raised within a predominantly negotiating atmosphere. We may have to get more used to asking open rather than closed questions, raising issues where stances are not rigid and positions have not been drawn up. Time will have to be allowed for such developments. The concept of continuous education will perhaps have to be accepted more as a living reality than an unachievable dream.

Such developments can easily be misunderstood and become ensnared in traps and given labels such as 'welfarism', 'human relations' and 'managerialism' which not only denies their essential nature but can reduce them to mere parodies of their real purpose. If this is a real danger then certain acid tests can be built into the system to test the seriousness of intentions in the social area. For example, how many organizations are currently willing to face the economic versus social choice of declaring redundancies or keeping men on in an over-manned situation in order to avoid possible social consequences?

3 A behavioural as well as a structural dimension
Changes in rules, structures and systems cannot be undertaken without necessary behavioural changes. For example the appointment of safety representatives or worker directors will not work without:

the necessary skill/knowledge being built up
the associated climate change—from negotiation to consultation, conflict to cooperation, bargaining to problem solving, being facilitated.

This process will be helped by calling on the experiences of those concerned through the operation of joint bodies such as joint committees, briefing groups and representative systems. This experience needs to be used, not just allowed to happen. The ability to learn from experience through working on the issues which arise needs to be built up. The way in which things are done as well as what is done needs to be considered and learning related to awareness expansion, group and relationship activities needs to be promoted on the basis of sound initial training.

4 Third party involvement
Problems may be too complex and demanding for the principal parties themselves to sort out on their own without outside help. This especially applies at initial stages where the processes of information generation and handling need care and skill in managing especially if confidential or sensitive views or opinions have been expressed. Organizations are increasingly open to the environment with which they are faced and are therefore perhaps less reluctant to use external resources. Using outside help sparingly can be a sign of strength

therefore and an indication of good faith. the methods to use here therefore are perhaps contacts with outside institutions such as the Advisory, Conciliation and Arbitration Service (ACAS), external resources such as consultants and the amount of exchange of personnel with other organizations which is encouraged. How would your organization measure up to these criteria?

5 *A broad view of conflict*

Are there enough channels through which to deal effectively with the types of conflict which are likely to arise within the operations of most organizations? Simple systems like collective bargaining only fit simple problems. Complex problems require elaborated systems and increased 'redundancy' in terms of communication channels. Some examples of the necessary channels which might be required are:

Representative systems—is there a recognized shop steward for every 20–25 members? Is there a shop stewards committee where there are more than (say) 12 shop stewards? Is there a full time convenor for more than 20 stewards, or companies above 500 employees?

Communication channels—eg briefing groups

Appraisal systems

Confrontation meetings—eg discussions on a particular issue or annual 'hair down' sessions

Project teams—eg introducing a job evaluation scheme

Learning groups—eg 'action learning' groups of managers and shop stewards.

6 *A range of conflict resolution methods*

As well as the normal bargaining and consultative methods does the capability exist for dealing with conflict in less orthodox ways? How easy is it for subordinates to tell their bosses that they disagree with them—how often does this happen in practice? How many times are managers wrong but get away with it because their subordinates are too frightened or bosses too remote to draw attention to it? The ability to admit weakness and express open behaviour is often the first step towards a more free relationship. How far are you along this route towards resolving conflicts? This capacity sometimes may need to be formalized in some way to make sure that the cathartic effects do not spill over. All too often conflict can be destructive anyway without raising the temperature unnecessarily. It may require skill and patience to clear the ground effectively for underlying assumptions of managerial omnipotence and union nihilism to be questioned! The potential rewards are high in terms of reaching out to the real problems of substance beneath the thin veneer of industrial relations activity for those brave and skilful enough to try.

Six major strategy points have been highlighted which we consider are vital if a development approach to industrial relations is to be effectively introduced. Some key questions have been posed, the answers to which give vital clues to the propensity for development in any organization. What answers would your organization give? Dare *you* ask the questions?

B APPRAISAL

Marjo van Boeschoten

Although appraisal as a widely used management tool has been with us for more than a decade, many doubts are still expressed about its validity and the contribution it makes to organizational efficiency and effectiveness. In this article the author draws on his considerable experience of appraisal systems to show the fundamental inadequacies of most approaches. He suggests how the system could be made more meaningful by taking the age of the appraisee as a factor in discussing performance. Marjo van Boeschoten further argues that age makes some unique demands on the individual and reasons that, by rejecting or ignoring those demands, the organization misses some vital data on the developmental requirements of the individual concerned.

INTRODUCTION

In one week recently I heard managers from different companies raise the same questions about appraisal:

'But if I have no system of appraisal how shall I be able to determine what people should earn?'

'If I have two salesmen, one of 58 and one of 25, both doing the same job, there seems something wrong in having to use the same form and the same yardsticks for their appraisal.'

These two questions seem indicative of two basic issues in relation to appraisal:

what are the effects of linking an appraisal system to financial reward?

to what extent should a system of appraisal take account of age or of the different development characteristics and problems belonging to certain periods of life?

There is also a third question which will be discussed in this chapter. Most appraisal systems are based on the necessity of judging people's behaviour over a period. I should like to go into the question of the effect judging people has on human relationships and development and how that relates to the activity of giving feedback.

It is necessary to say from the outset that any readers who are hoping for some kind of comprehensive, simple appraisal system to replace their present inadequate one may be disappointed. This chapter will not be about systems but about assumptions and values underlying systems, and about possible new approaches to the question of appraisal. Some guidance for improving appraisal in practice will be provided.

THE LINK WITH PAYMENT

In many modern companies we find that a distinction is increasingly made between appraisal interviews and career review and planning interviews. In the appraisal interview the main emphasis is on judging past performance, so that through some system of points rating there will be consequences for the level of pay in the coming period. The career planning and review interview has no direct bearing upon future income and is usually concerned with a longer time span. The fact that management has felt the need to create these two separate entities is an indication of the limitations of the appraisal system which has a link with payment. We do not usually find appraisal systems that have a direct link with payment for higher levels of employee. They are most commonly found in the case of:

shopfloor workers, where they have replaced cruder forms of quantity-based incentive schemes

white collar workers up to the level of middle management sales representatives.

The two main reasons for having appraisal systems of this nature are:

to establish a fair and objective method of rewarding good performance
for management to acquire information for career planning.

These seem perfectly sound and reasonable motives. 'A fair day's pay for a fair day's work' is still one of the most accepted values of our present society. But in practice there are difficulties in realizing this principle. First, it has become increasingly difficult to determine and to agree on the content of 'a fair day's work'. With the greater complexity of our technology and the structure of our organizations, it has become almost impossible to measure a fair day's work on a purely quantitative basis. Qualitative factors of attitudes and behaviour are an integral part of total job performance. Assessing these requires the weighing of qualitative values against objective yardsticks that are far more difficult to develop or to get agreement on. This issue is often dodged by creating an 'impression' of objectivity in using a points scale in relation to the measurement of human behaviour or character qualities. Issues like 'leadership' (whatever the interpretation of that may be), 'initiative', and also less vague matters like 'quality of merchandising' for a salesman, are put against a points scale of 1 to 10. Their assessment is then given a semblance of objectivity by them being scored as 6 rather than something like 'in my judgement not terribly good'. The designers of such systems recognize the obvious inadequacy of misprocedure and urge the users to support their numerical judgements with additional facts. This still leaves the question of how many facts of what nature will lead to what judgement, to how many points and how much money! The number of variables is immense and the main variable is still the judgement of the individual manager, his life experience, his personal hang-ups and his mood of the day.

'Defending' judgements to subordinates is a task that managers do not usually look forward to. They cannot avoid the issue by giving high marks to all and sundry because this policy will eventually come to the notice of others. Alternatively, a manager cannot give very low marks, consistently if he is to maintain a reasonable relationship with his subordinates. As a result what we usually see is managers aiming for the safe middle ground, so as not to transgress in either way, thereby making the exercise quite meaningless.

Some companies have responded to this situation by compelling their managers to have the total outcome of their appraisal results comply with the curve of Gauss (a normal distribution) demonstrating a distribution of qualities that can be statistically justified. As far as I have been able to gather from managers who have been faced with this situation this results in them experiencing even more pressure and calls for the use of greater political skill.

Another question that has recently come more to the foreground concerns the extent to which it is still realistic to judge individual performance. One characteristic of complex organizations within a complex society is the high degree of interdependency of people trying to work towards a shared objective. There is virtually no aspect of our work today that is not dependent on the work and goodwill of others. In most appraisal systems we see that the factor of dependency on others has been eliminated from the judgement process and this again raises the question of fairness.

All the problems above show the difficulty of bringing into practice the principle of a fair year's reward for a fair year's work on an individual basis. These problems also make it clear that it is virtually impossible to use data of this nature as a reliable basis for career planning. The whole issue has been clouded by the imprecision of qualitative measurements and the need for justification of judgements.

In some companies appraisal systems are still seen by management as an incentive to work. It is the old carrot and stick principle, this time applied with slightly more sophistication perhaps but still with the assumption that people are basically lazy and lack inner motivation. I will not go into the evidence on how people can become skilled in 'playing' various kinds of incentive systems so as to bring them into line with their own aims rather than management's. This has been made clear by others on various occasions.[52] But I think it may still be worthwhile just to draw notice to the fact these systems can become self-defeating by making people pay-oriented rather than work-oriented. (I am of course well aware of the many work situations that provide little inner motivation for the holders of the job. This is a complex structural and social problem but I am convinced that the ultimate solution does not lie in replacing a structural lack of inner motivation by external incentives. On the contrary this stop-gap seems to delay the activity of facing the real problem.)

If the incentive theory does not appear to be on very firm ground either, is there still a case for sustaining the appraisal system which is linked to pay? In my opinion the answer is no.

Management generally gets paid for the job it is asked to do without extras for personal performance. Why could it not be the same for other people? If people do particularly well that is a reason to give them more responsibility and more money as a direct consequence. If the company has done well as a consequence of good cooperation between management and workers they can all then share in the benefits of that collaboration. That is not a carrot but a good meal after a good day's work. The meal was not the aim of the work but the end of a good day. If people do not do well, management should look into the reasons for this with the people concerned with a view to correction and improvement.

Payment is for the job, for the responsibility that is given to people. It can also take into account the varying needs of people according to their age and stage of development in life. We still have to be aware of a competitive element. Many people still want more money for a job done better than others have done it. They want this as a recognition of the results they have achieved. But that is a consequence of the very system we created for employees in those levels of the organization. It is the self-fulfilling prophecy of the carrot and stick approach. Higher levels of management can experience the satisfaction of a job well done for the sake of the job itself. In addition, perhaps they also get the prospect of an even more interesting job to grow out of it. There is no reason why managers with imagination could not create a similar situation for the levels below them. For example, younger people in particular like to compare with others because they still have a strong need to establish their own values. This holds a challenge and an opportunity for management—how to give these young people tasks and assignments of a challenging nature that will give them the chance to compare with themselves rather than with others!

Despite all the problems and reservations, I believe that a system of regular evaluation and planning of people's development in relation to their work remains essential. In a more mature working environment let us hope that we shall get out of the habit of handing out reports to people and get down to the real business: of showing serious application to the task of continuously developing our human resources.

Taking account of man as a developing being

If we see it as management's responsibility to support and promote people's development in their jobs and in the company, that means we take responsiblity for three issues:

the structure and 'environment' of the job
the man, his strengths and weaknesses, his potential
the relationship between the two.

I will not enter into the question of job structure and environment, because it would go beyond the remit of this chapter and in any case, the subject is covered by Eric Mitchell later on. I will however make occasional references to this issue, when I enter more deeply into the question of what the significance of work is to people of different age groups.

My starting point is that management has a basically unchanging expectation on how it wants a job to be performed, whereas people have something different to offer to the job and to take from the job. To give a simple example: I have had some experience working as a docker. In the group I worked in, there was a wide spread of ages. Management expected so many tons a day and the group, (whether or not they were trying to meet that target), divided the workload amongst its members. Older people had to be (and were) very economical in the use of their bodies but were still given more breathing space by their colleagues than the younger, stronger persons. One could distinguish three basic roles within the group:

the younger group shifting most of the tonnage
a middle group that was good at getting things organized
and an older group that looked after the morale of the group and often
provided a useful protective 'umbrella' against the various pressures
coming from the supervisors.

Nobody ever discussed with them how they were developing in relation to their job but one could see how, according to age, they were relating differently to what was seen by management as just one (very simple) kind of job. According to age range quite a different quality was given to the job. There are of course, many jobs that do not provide this kind of opportunity. However it would surely be better if, in the cases where it did apply, there were some form of recognition by management of the different qualities that are brought to the job by different age groups. It would be similarly beneficial if management took account of what the job might contribute to the worker's personal development in terms of age.

How then could the tool of appraisal contribute to a more balanced approach to development, one that takes account of the needs of the job as well as of the needs of the man? For that we need to look more closely at the specific needs and problems of different age groups.

Early and middle 20s age group—this group of young adults is still very much in the process of entering the world, trying to find its own feet and wanting to find out a great deal more about itself. The attitude of the young adult is expansive. He want to assert himself, make himself visible. This outward behaviour stems from his inner search for the answer to three questions, Who am I? What do I want? and What can I do? In order to find out about himself he needs the world as a mirror. The more different pictures he can see the more he can discover about himself. In work terms, this means a lot of varied experience, in different jobs, preferably with a gradual growth of responsibility. Nothing is more deadly for the development of human potential than for young adults to be placed in unchallenging routine jobs or to specialize them quickly within their (academic) discipline. The other aspect is that not only should there be many mirrors but the mirrors should also speak. Very clear feedback on how this behaviour has affected others is called for. This should be given, in an undisguised manner but in a mood of objectivity. This can help the young adult to find out about his boundaries, about his aims and his direction. Young people do not usually think in terms of a long time span, so feedback should be given regularly and it should relate to recent events. At less frequent intervals a discussion on the future would be meaningful, particularly if the person is helped to formulate his own targets for the near future against the background of what the company might require of him.

Late 20s to middle 30s—by this time most people have acquired a certain confidence in their abilities. There are two main needs, to widen the social horizon and to deepen relationships with people and with work. So this is the best time for specialization and for taking on a wider responsibility. This is also the age where people develop a more rational relationship to their environment. They are less preoccupied with themselves and therefore more free to take a more detached view of the situation of which they are part. Organizational and analytical tasks are very suitable for this age group.

Nowadays the image we present to others is an important issue for many people. Fromm speaks about 'the marketing image' and says that people experience themselves both as the seller and the commodity they have to sell. Particularly in their early 30s, people can experience anxiety about their identity as it has become unclear which is the real self and which the adapted role.

In appraisal terms people of this age group are most interested in being helped to make a clear analysis of their activities of the last few years and of the career they see before them. They should be strongly encouraged to think in terms of active career planning rather than waiting for the company to do the planning for them. What can you do to become a more professional person? What investment in time and energy are you prepared to make for your own development? Are you sure about your direction? What help would you like to get from the company? Those are the type of questions that are meaningful at this point.

Middle 30s to early 40s—as people approach 40 the concept (and often fear) of middle age becomes a reality. Doubts about the value of what one has become and uncertainty about what might still remain ahead lies at the back of people's thoughts. There is a tendency to ignore or suppress these feelings, often resulting in outbursts of great energy or activity. It is important for human development that these questions are faced as this period might be regarded as a preparation for a new birth of the self. There is an opportunity for an individual to establish his real tasks in life, both in relation to what may be perceived as the needs of his environment and to what he as an individual might have to offer to the world. Particularly in their early 40s people begin to look for a new quality in their lives, for aims and activities that are more inspiring or exciting than those of the past. It is often the time for a last change of job, in that such a move could still be made without too high a risk.

It is important that managers, in relating to these (often not expressed) questions faced by their subordinates, should find the time to discuss them in greater depth with the individuals concerned. Depending on the nature of the relationship people might feel free to express some of their anxieties and these could then be translated into questions of a more positive nature, such as, 'What is important to you now? What kind of life do you see before you? How do we see the company (or your department) developing and what opportunities does that offer to you? If we do not see a real possibility of a change of job, could there be a change of role within your job which might make it more interesting?'

Making a significant change at this stage might not be a bad thing for individuals but if this now represents only an attempt to escape from these existential questions then it might very likely prove to be detrimental both in terms of the development of the person and the future contribution he might make to the organization.

Middle and late 40s—this can be the period where people who have worked with the questions of the previous period show and experience a new enthusiasm for their work. There is less of a need to be seen to do well and more a need to do a job that is meaningful to others and to the situation. People at this stage would not feel defensive towards a young generation but would enjoy helping them to get on with their tasks in life.

However, there will be another group as well within this age bracket. Our present society does not particularly encourage people to take time out for themselves. For many people, particularly those who had had little opportunity to find out about themselves in their 20s, it is hard work to create some new meaningful aims for themselves. Such people become increasingly defensive and hardened, resistant to change, demonstrative of their power and strengths and, as they grow old, they increasingly becoming a source of irritation for others and eventually a (tragic) laughing stock for a younger generation. For both groups (and the many others in between these two extremes) there is now also the issue of coming to terms with the reality of the finality of life. The degree of acceptance of the fact of death will have a profound effect on the amount of stress and tension people experience in their daily life. The more it is accepted, the more relaxed the attitude to life seems to become and the more time people seem to have.

One can see that discussions about past and future work development will have to be very different for these two categories. For the more mature people the discussion would focus primarily on issues and problems of the environment of which he is part and the contribution he could make to improve the situation or the help he could give to colleagues. For the more regressive people it might be helpful to ask them how they see the effect they are having on their environment and how they feel about the response they are receiving. In relation to the future, it would be wise to avoid shaking any admonishing fingers. It would be much more helpful to ask what alternatives they see for their own future development and what they perceive as the consequences of these alternatives.

The 50s—from the point of view of appraisal there is little more to be said about this group in addition to what has been said about the previous group. People with a mature attitude to life and to themselves will continue to make a valuable contribution to the organization. Regardless of their jobs, they might bring the qualities of wisdom and compassion to daily working life and, at more managerial levels, their social and conceptual skills, their vision in the area of policy design and implementation can be great assets to any company. They are the best people to help others orient themselves. For those in the more regressive group it requires serious consideration concerning how they can still make the best possible contribution and where they can cause the least possible damage to others. One option might be for them to move to more specialized work areas which demand that they interact less with others.

A particular consideration should perhaps be given to the physical aspects, especially for people in their late and middle 50s. With hard physical labour it is obvious that the older man will expend relatively more of his available energy on his daily work than a younger man carrying out the same tasks. To take this seriously means (as I indicated with my example from the docks) that management would have to think about the possibility of formalizing certain role-aspects of the job, that would take off some of the physical workload. For less physical work we need to be aware of the much greater stress people with a defensive and anxious personality live under. They are threatened most by coronaries and other forms of sudden collapse. If the company has a medical service there is the possibility that a trusted company doctor could do much to prevent these disasters from happening in discussing causes of stress with the person who begins to show signs of concern about his health.

Approaching retirement—in the last few years of working life an appraisal of the past year's working performance can become a nonsense. Even if people were interested in taking part in such a review (which in itself is quite unlikely), the effect it might still have on their future performances would in any case be negligible. There are two issues that might still be meainingfully discussed:

the process of handing over the job to others
preparation for retirement

The more mature personality would have little difficulty handing over to others. The discussion here would be mainly on what the company might do to facilitate this process. The more hardened person would find it difficult to hand over and others would have to help him to become aware of his responsibility by pointing out the consequences of his holding on.

Again, with the more fully developed personality, there will not be too much of a problem in preparing for the time of retirement. He will usually have thought about the future content of his life long before the actual moment of retirement is there. For the more anxious personality, work very often has become the main justification for his existence and in such cases the moment of retirement takes away the essential meaning of life. It is a common phenomenon that people who had been active and energetic right up to retirement age often physically deteriorate soon after. Here the company has the opportunity to help people prepare for retirement by discussing with them various alternatives that they might see for filling their lives after retirement. It is the counterpart of the process of induction. Preparing people for leaving working life is perhaps the last responsibility of management towards its human resources.

JUDGING PEOPLE VERSUS GIVING FEEDBACK

A very good, older friend of mine said to me a few years ago, 'You know, I have found more and more that I no longer have to judge people. I cannot tell you how much joy that gives me.' I was not quite sure at the time that I had understood what he meant but gradually over the years this thought has acquired more meaning for me. I began to look how my own judging of people was affecting me and my relationship to people. In working with groups I found that I usually gained a certain impression of the image people presented to me during a first working day. If I translated this image for myself into a judgment, so ascribing certain qualities to these other people, very often I found that the relationship that had developed between myself and these people would confirm the image I had made of them at the end of the first day's meeting. No matter how I behaved, no matter how much I concealed any negative judgements of them, the development of the relationship would be blocked by the pictures, the labels I had inwardly conferred upon them.

I found that in looking beyond what people were presenting to me in their behaviour, in not just looking at what people had become, but also at the individuality behind that (one might say what the person is trying to become) it was then that I found a real opportunity of meeting people and developing a relationship. It is in gaining this freedom, the choice of keeping an open mind towards people, in experiencing a mixture of wonder and respect for the real self behind the presented image that I discovered this same quality of joy that my friend told me about.

People sense when we hold judgements over them and this is so even if these judgements are not openly expressed. They usually react defensively when they are presented with these judgements. Telling people what they are like, what (negative) qualities they have (in our opinion), leads to a closing off and hardly ever to an opening up of interest or an urge to explore on the part of the recipient. Even telling people what good or wonderful qualities they have will produce not much more than a brief sense of gratification and a feeling of 'so what?' in the listener. Should we then be less direct and never tell people what we think about them? On the contrary, my feeling is that in the judgemental kind of appraisal interview there is often a great deal of unnecessary avoiding of painful issues. This is mainly because managers dislike the emotional reactions and defensive situations which result from such judgements. Real facts and feelings are not openly expressed but judgements are made and conveyed in a less direct, strictly rational way. This can be more distressing than a direct approach.

CONCLUSION

Appraisal interviews have learning as an aim, learning from the past and in preparation for the future. Learning can be gained in evaluating past events, past behaviour and the effect behaviour has had on others and the situation at hand. The manager who conducts the interview should sit not in judgement but should act as a facilitator of learning, so helping the interviewee to gain insight into what has happened in the past period and what his role had been in those events. 'What happened? What did you do? What effect did this have on the situation and on other people? Could you have acted differently? How? What have you learned from the past period? Where are you now in your development?

Where do you want to go? Is that realistic? What are the next steps then for the coming period?

These are the type of questions that are helpful to explore in an appraisal interview and it has been my experience that people can take part successfully in such self-reviews. This opens up the way for further learning if the interview is conducted in an exploratory objective way.

Finally, we do of course have blind spots; there are always certain areas that we do not like to look at because we fear that they may be too hurtful for our self-image. Anxiety about these areas can cause more harm than the act of facing the present reality. This is where an appraisal can help by giving feedback on how we experienced that situation, on the effect that the other person's behaviour had on us. 'The picture is my picture. It may be wrong because of my bias, but it is the best I can give you. It may be painful, but it is the reality I believe you might have to face. If you could accept it, you could work on it and we would be able to assess what help you would like to receive for it.' Therein lies the difference between judgement and feedback. The person who gives the kind of feedback as pictured above remains open and vulnerable in the situation. That is where real learning can take place and where the working relationship has further development opportunities.

C TRAINING

John Bristow and Rod Scarth

In recent times training as a specialism has been at the forefront of human resource management. Yet we often train people without asking what the individual's own needs and expectations are. The validity and effectiveness of training is sometimes highly suspect and we fail to take account of answers to even the most basic questions, such a· what are we training people for? how should the programme be designed? who should be involved? and how are we going to ensure that trainees do not feel that they are being trained by the man in the training centre?

In this paper the authors argue that, in order to minimize some of these ills, we need to understand the principles of a developmental approach to training. John Bristow and Rod Scarth not only enumerate these principles in some detail but also show how they can be used by giving two company-based case studies which record their own recent experiences.

We shall outline in this paper some of the main principles, assumptions and values underlying a developmental approach to training and then go on to illustrate the implications of these principles for planning and implementing strategies for training.

SOME PRINCIPLES DERIVED FROM A DEVELOPMENTAL APPROACH TO TRAINING

1 *The learning objectives come from real problems and issues*

The purpose of development is different from that of training. The aim of training may quite rightly be to fit people to a prescribed role and equip them with necessary knowledge and skill. The aim of development is to provide the situations and conditions for people to develop themselves through the content of their life experience rather than through acquiring something from other people, such as knowledge and skill, though this is necessary too. For this, objectives must emerge out of that life experience, ie out of the needs, aspirations and problems in the current situation. The developmental approach is to use current problems and issues as the vehicle or opportunity for learning. The actual process of solving problems and adapting to change can provide the necessary experiences for learning to occur. Hence feedback and surveys are used to bring people face to face with their current realities, rather than to analyse training needs around which the trainer designs a course. In relating directly to immediate issues, the developmental approach differs from much conventional training. This may follow historical precedents and often, partly to save work, the training programmes remain the same and are structured in advance so running the danger of being only partially related to the needs of those who come or are sent on a course. Sometimes conventional training departs from providing people with knowledge and skills for a job and, particularly at management level, implies some ideal stereotype of how managers should operate, with the trainer acting as the exponent of the desired values and behaviour. It is not surprising if some managers then think of training as 'doing something to people', creating desirable attitudes or changing 'difficult' employees. For development, on the other hand, the trainer aims at creating a setting in which people feel free and are encouraged to change but are in no way pressurized.

2   *A collaborative contract between the trainer, manager and trainee on goals, methods and responsibilities*
As the objectives of development emerge from the current situation directly, it is easier for them to be set collaboratively. Where in conventional training objectives are set by senior management for those lower in the hierarchy, in a development exercise the needs of the situation are explored by all those concerned together. Instead of thinking that training others may be a panacea for their problems, managers can check to see if this is not avoiding the real issues. They might also find that they need to change and learn as well as their staff. Together they draw up a picture of the desired state for the future, that is, the training objectives. This mutual recognition of needs and identification of goals is itself part of the learning process and through participation there is a strong ownership of and commitment to the goals.

Coming to a contract and shared understanding over the design and methods of training can be harder. This is mainly because trainees and managers come with different expectations of what training is and how learning occurs. By gradual changes in structuring and methods, the trainer can help all parties to recognize the processes of learning and the factors that help and hinder it.

The final part of the contract is a realistic mutual understanding of the responsibilities of each party involved. Management might normally expect that the trainer alone is responsible for the total learning process. The trainer must then bring the managers and trainees to see where each of them is responsible, and so lay the foundation of a collaborative relationship. For example, everyone might be responsible for ensuring that training is related to real needs; the trainer mainly responsible for the design of the training itself; but the manager and his trainees mainly responsible for the transfer back into the real life situation, with the trainer providing conditions that help this. Transfer is often assumed to occur spontaneously and if it does not it is the trainer's fault.

3 Learning takes place within ongoing work relationships or groups

Often managers do not realize that they or the organization of their department will have to change as their own staff learn, change and develop. Learning is thought to occur only in individuals separately. It is forgotten that role and norms and social pressures affect performance as much as knowledge, skills and attitudes. Often course members return home enthusiastic to apply new insights and skills only to meet with resistance and feel out of context. The OD approach is to bring changes of roles, norms and structures into the process of learning by training people together with those with whom they actually work. This enables learning to be transferred and integrated into the work and social context more easily. Members of the group learn from each other. Perceptions, expectations and attitudes of people towards each other change. The group learns that it can do things differently and that it is acceptable to behave that way. Managers learn from and through their own staff. As a number of groups learn this way it is possible to speak of organizational learning and development. What is socially built up and maintained can only be socially changed and transformed. That means working with the whole work group and other groups with which it is in contact. When doing this it is essential to look at the whole social system within which the group operates (a factory, office or unit) and the relationships existing within the system. Then it is possible to judge which groups and levels to start with and on what tasks and issues.

4 Learning is seen as a total process in itself, involving all aspects of human experience

Training is often work rather than life based. People may be seen only in relation to money and production, as means for these ends. With the developmental approach, learning is seen in the context of the whole person and all the areas of life rather than a particular skill or role that is being performed. Training addresses itself to the whole man (thought, feelings, values and action), rather than just a part of him. This broadens the focus of the training and learning objectives so that they might well include interests, energy, feelings, values and relationships as well as knowledge, skills and attitudes.

Just as there may be only a partial or simple model of man, so there can be an oversimplified view of the learning process. Knowledge and thinking are expected to lead to action. Feelings and emotions are usually neglected. The social context in which learning is to manifest itself is largely ignored. In designing the structure of a training event, the learning process is seen as an organic totality with certain phases and steps in which all the different parts of man are involved (thinking, feeling and action) each balancing the other in sequence. There is attention given to both the work task and the relationships, the process and the structure, the person and the role, feedback and conceptualization of past experience on the one hand, and goal setting and future planning on the other. The approach would be to build up a whole competence in an area (eg interpersonal competence) rather than a skill or bit of information on its own (eg social skills training). The methods vary according to whether the emphasis at that moment is on concepts, perception, skills, relationships, feelings and motivation. Didactic and experiential components are balanced.

5 Trainees direct their own learning

Often people become passive or dependent during a training course and expect or demand answers. They revert back to their behaviour at school and expect to be taught like children. The trainer adopting an OD approach would be more concerned with helping people learn how to learn. He will ensure that the trainee understands, owns and directs the focus of the training. This requires an active response from the trainee. He needs to seek questions rather than answers and to establish an interdependent relationship with the trainer. Where assessment is brought into learning it is in the form of feedback rather than judgement, encouraging self-confrontation and self-assessment by the trainee. Adults, it is assumed, learn differently from children as they are capable of greater responsiblity and judgement and self-direction. Also, learning in reality is clearly a struggle or effort, and this becomes apparent as trainees learn that they have to acquire something themselves and cannot be handed it on a plate.

6 Training as the mangement of different kinds of learning

There are many different qualities of experience that can be part of what is called 'learning'. There is conditioning and the learning of automatic behaviour and attitudes. When working mainly with this end in view the trainer is an instructor. In a developmental approach to instruction, the trainer would address the man as a man rather than an organism to be circus trained. He would cooperate with him in so far as he chooses to undergo instruction to learn a skill or fulfil a role. A sequence of experiences can be systematically organized when the tasks are predictable and the knowledge, skills or perception required can be thoroughly analysed. The steps to build up skill or refine perception can be logically ordered and the methods evaluated against outcome.

Informal conditioning will be part of any learning process just as it is part of the dynamic of any group or organization. But there are other aspects to learning. There are open-ended situations where trainees need to learn how to be more sensitive to materials, machines, themselves, other people or the way organizations work. This brings them into contact with themselves and their environment and enables them to act and relate more intelligently. The trainer encourages them to be free enough from their expectations, preoccupations and defences to see, hear, sense or feel something new for themselves. This can lead on to a further stage when the trainee knows what he is experiencing and doing in the moment and is not caught up in it. At such moments he can judge his progress, know what he has to struggle with, direct his own learning and experience full understanding. Ultimately, learning becomes a creative experience for both trainee and trainer. The aim then is to create a situation in which these qualities enter experience. The trainer is more of an educator than an instructor. He is a guide or catalyst in the process of learning and he is there to help the trainees see what they need and to learn what they did not expect to learn. Learning to learn is like learning a process without predictable content, cues or responses.

Training then is the management of different kinds of learning. The trainer has to adapt to the needs of the moment—asking Socratic questions and encouraging communication; illustrating concepts and demonstrating skills; introducing structure or letting things develop. Whether instructor or educator, the trainer has to establish a collaborative relationship with the trainees for real exchange to occur. To do this the trainer has not only to be sensitive to the trainee but also aware of his own needs and values. He has to strive to relate as impartially as possible to people and organizations with values different from his own and to respond from understanding rather than from a 'position'.

7 Integrating the training function within the organization

Often training is on the periphery of an organization, having very little influence. People may be posted into training because they are unable to function successfully elsewhere. With an OD approach, training will be seen to be relating successfully to management and employee problems, and will then gain in importance. But if the values of the training department are not shared by line management and the social system is seen as very much secondary to production and marketing, then the OD approach is to bring managers to see how the social system is important and how the management of people requires sound, clear values and understanding. As corporate policy begins to provide for the development of human resources on an equal footing with the economic and technical, training will become an integrated part of day to day activity. This will become more so as managers have more of an understanding of the learning process and the trainer's role. They will become involved in the planning and implementation of training, responsibility for training being increasingly shared with line management. The training function may be less centralized as local training and development councils meet to review the changing needs of the organization and of individuals, through feedback from appraisal interviews. Training then will not only be meeting the needs to maintain the system (eg fitting people to jobs) but also helping the system develop, through adapting to change, solving problems, improving relations between functions or within teams, making policies and altering structures. Training and learning become inseparable from organizational change.

8 *Work becomes a place where people learn and develop*

If training is carried on away from the workplace and people are being put through experiences and taught ideas that do not relate directly to their needs, it does not help to build up a climate or 'culture' at the place of work where people learn from each other on the job. This is one of the ultimate aims in OD. This means building norms and customs whereby people give each other feedback on their performance or the way their behaviour is affecting others. They also ask and give help to each other, and teach each other their knowledge and skills. These norms can only be established through creating effective relationships and teams on the shop floor, in the office or in the boardroom. Learning can then carry on outside training or other forms of institutionalized learning. The balance between learning through life on the job and learning through experiences in an organized set of activities must be kept. Learning can never be really divorced from life.

Two examples of these principles in action

The first example illustrates a strategy of training that involved the line management in a change process using supervisory training. After a training needs survey the board of the company decided that it needed to invest considerable time and effort in improving the expertise of supervisors in managing their jobs. Some of the findings of the survey that had led to this conclusion were that supervisors had in recent years lost their traditional role characterized by hiring and firing, direct responsibility for the labour force, etc; with the increasing complexity of industry and in particular the increasing power of the trade unions, supervisors were ill-equipped to cope with the demands of the job; many workers were seen to be under-supervised; managers did more and more of the administrative work, supervisors' status had declined. This survey had identified a need which was common throughout the company, and had enabled senior management to recognize this, and give its sanction to an investment of time and effort. This was part of the process of establishing a contract between the training function and the rest of the company.

In response to these problems a strategy was drawn up to develop a programme of activities. A number of factors had to be considered in the strategic thinking, both constraints and helping factors. On the constraints side the company was highly traditional in the sense that the technical process had not fundamentally altered since 1880 and, with the company cushioned from external technical pressures, the management had not felt the need to adapt to change. The assumptions about how to manage people were still rooted in those of 'scientific management' (managing people was seen to be the same as managing a technical or mechanical process) and this made managers and supervisors all the more ill-prepared for change. Increasing company size had led to alienation and increasing inefficiency which top management responded to by looking to the external environment for salvation in the form of takeovers and diversification. On the helping side, the managing director was increasingly aware of the social and political forces compelling change in industry. The anticipation of impending government legislation (eg 'Let's get to work now and beat the legislation') and a real fear of the power of worker directors provided the initial impetus. A senior policy making group was established which after two years' deliberations produced a *list* of areas needing consideration in the employee relations field. The supervisors came at the top of the list. The company was being restructured to enable decisions to be made more locally. Another major factor affecting strategy was the lack of training resources available, with one trainer to cover 27 sites. The aim was to train all 435 supervisors in the company over two years. In forming a strategy it is most useful to look at the forces that help and hinder change in the direction indicated by the objectives and needs.

The programme was initiated by joint meetings of both managers and supervisors from each of the five company regions and the two subsidiary companies, with two representatives of each coming from regions covering a wide area. The aim of these meetings was for supervisors and managers to exchange views on the problems supervisors were having in their jobs and then for both to develop objectives and plans with the trainer for solving these problems. Three questions were asked: What were the real problems faced by supervisors in their jobs as seen by supervisors, by managers and by operatives? How can the situation be put to rights again given our limited resources? Who is responsible for doing this? The goal was to agree by the end of the meeting the aims, content, structure, follow-up and resources for supervisory training. It is worth noting the strategy in holding these meetings, and the principles implied by this strategy. The meeting involved both the manager and his staff for whom the training was intended. They were encouraged to look at real problems (rather than making assumptions about the need for training) by the trainer asking pertinent questions and helping them appreciate each others' perceptions. Three parties were concerned in the decision on objectives and methods: the managers, their staff and the trainer. One party was not imposing on the other. The trainer broke through any existing assumptions about the trainer's responsibility for learning or training, and about 'training' as a 'cure' for problems, by asking about who would really be responsible for what at each stage in the training.

The managers and supervisors present at the meeting decided that the objectives of the supervisors training programme should be threefold: to help the supervisor to see more clearly what his role is and what it could be and to develop plans with his own manager; to provide information on new employment legislation to update supervisors' knowledge; and to make supervisors sensitive to each other through human relations training. They drew up a plan in four parts or stages to meet these objectives. Part 1 covering legislation and the supervisor's role and part 2 concentrating on human relations training, would together form a two and a half day course for supervisors. Part 3 would be a joint two day meeting between a manager and his own supervisory team to develop further plans to integrate learning into the job and to discuss ways in which the supervisory team needed to develop its own team operation. Part 4 would be a follow up by personnel and training managers to discuss what further work may be necersary. There are some significant features of the objectives and plans. The aims and focus formed a natural progression that increasingly involved the whole person, from legislation to role to social skills and competence to team building and problem solving. Part 3, building the management and supervisory team and planning how to integrate and implement the training in everyday life, is uncommon in conventional training and characterizes the OD approach. The team building provides learning within the context of actual work relationships and enables lasting changes to take place in these relationships, with both the supervisor and his boss planning together how to integrate the training into life. The responsibility for transfer was seen to be theirs, so increasing the chances of implementing any actual changes as a result of the training. The natural stages of the training programme from inception to implementation formed an organic totality and learning never lost touch with actual work problems or relationships.

Another unusual feature of the training strategy was that a decision was made at the planning meeting that a trainer would run each supervisors course jointly with two or three line managers. The managers would be the trainers of their own supervisors and the trainer would be there only as a back-up resource. This meant that before this took place the managers had to go through a four day course to learn how to train others in these areas. So the programme decided at the joint meeting was as follows: the managers were trained to be trainers; they then briefed their supervisors on the training course; they ran the course with a trainer present; they then met in a team with their supervisors to improve team functioning and to see what changes could be made as a result of the learning; a follow-up visit was made by the trainer. In addition to being responsible for the objective setting and planning at the beginning of the training programme and the implementation and team building at the end, the managers were partially responsible for the training sessions themselves. It is a characteristic of the OD approach to clarify the managers' responsibilities during the learning process. It is unusual though for the manager to be a trainer too, though he may attend the training itself. This complete involvement of the managers in the training of their supervisors had a number of effects, intended as part of the strategy. The managers had a far greater understanding of what training was all about, and the practices and principles behind it, and above all a very high commitment from being involved all the way through. This strategy had brought them into contact with supervisors at each stage. This understanding, contact and commitment was of enormous value when it came to the team building with the supervisors in Part 3.

The method used on the supervisors course were heavily dependent on set exercises. In OD terms this was regarded as a far from satisfactory situation. But with the limited number of trainers available and with the managers themselves doing training for the first time, it seemed that these more structured methods were necessary. It was a compromise but the gains in having the managers involved outweighed the losses from using set exercises. Set exercises might have discouraged trainees from asking questions and directing their own learning, and might mean that the higher levels of learning were not attained. But the team building that was to follow the training courses would allow for these qualities to enter the learning process.

The results are encouraging. The whole programme has not yet been completed as team building is just under way but several effects are already being noticed. The line managers are deeply committed to training their supervisors and feel a responsibility for ensuring that learning and training continues. The supervisors have enormously appreciated the care that has been taken—'The first time I felt the company cared about us for years'. The programme has provided both managers and supervisors with a valuable and solid foundation of knowledge and skill to tackle real problems in the workplace through team development. At the team building stage the managers and supervisors have so taken on ownership of the development programme that in some cases they preferred to carry on their team development without a trainer present, asserting their independence. Apart from managers changing by feeling responsibility for developing people and also being competent to do so, there has also been a change in the way the training department is viewed in the organization. This has come about with the success of these training activities, with the training dealing with the problems that management feel and with management understanding the principles of training. As this grows it may be possible to develop training policies with a greater understanding and to establish corporate policies that include a concern for the human resources and the social system in the company.

The following example illustrates the relevance of OD principles to the development of industrial relations at local level. In this case both management and shop stewards were involved, so there were two 'client groups' and the relationship varied according to the degree of trust and conflict between them. The learning had therefore to be related to the kind of trust possible and the conditions for this, to the nature and causes of conflict and to the ways of handling it constructively.

The manager of a company's local branch employing about 350 employees was faced with a technological change affecting methods and manning. He decided to set up regular meetings with the shop stewards to discuss handling of change, hoping that in the long term this would lead to worker participation in the form of a branch council. After initial suspicion, the shop stewards welcomed this as an opportunity to talk over real problems with management and to find ways of protecting jobs and employment in a time of insecurity.

Objectives shared by both management and union were to handle change more effectively; to learn how to solve problems together and to cooperate on joint projects; and to build trust and understanding between management and union. This was symbolized in the name given to these meetings, 'the syndicate'. The management assured the union that 'procedures' for disputes would not be affected or undermined by these meetings and both sides recognized that certain issues could only be handled that way. This was very much a venture into the unknown, so after some nine months the help of a researcher was welcome. The branch manager needed to feel the support of higher management in taking these risks. He also wanted some improvement in the effectiveness of the meetings. The shop stewards wanted to be clear about each other's feelings and of the views of the membership. Senior management wanted some evaluation of the effects of these meetings on attitudes and on industrial relations as a whole on site. The researcher was to help them through feedback and evaluation.

A strategy had to be evolved in the context of the industrial relations on site. The first strategic question was whether to build cooperation or improve the handling of conflict. With a union that was constitutional rather than militant, and a management that recognized the union and was willing to talk and work with it rather than be autocratic, it was thought best first to build up the capacity to cooperate rather than to start with the ability to handle conflict. This meant that the syndicate would have to tackle tasks and agenda items which were of potential mutual benefit or which concerned the future rather than a live issue of the present. As trust and understanding developed, topics and issues involving conflict could be introduced. The technological change would be used as a vehicle for involving the union differently and for building a more multi-faceted relationship between union and management. Both the relationship and behaviour of people at the meetings could change while working on this task, and trust could be strengthened through achievement. The direction of these developments would be explored by both sides together, through surveys, feedback and review (action research). These new activities and relationships would lead later to more lasting structural changes for involvement in decision making (eg councils) as seemed fit rather than any system being imposed from the start. The shop floor would be involved through working on projects themselves (a shop floor equivalent of the syndicate), or through their problems being tackled by the syndicate in consultation with them. Any training needed would be done jointly with management and union in syndicate. In this way the learning and change process were seen as an organic totality and viewed in relation to the ongoing relationship, current problems and the social system as a whole.

The methods used to help the syndicate initially were surveys with feedback, and review discussions and videotape showings of actual meetings. The surveys of both syndicate members and of the workforce/membership were fed back to the syndicate. Quotations of syndicate members were used so that interpretation and analysis were left to them in accordance with the principles of self-assessment and self-directed learning. Comments were grouped according to whether they related to improving the meeting, aspects of relations (hopes, fears and commitment) or roles and responsibilities (communication with the workforce). In reviewing meetings and discussing the videotape, the researcher asked them questions, getting them to say what they saw. This helped to raise their sensitivity and their perceptiveness and encouraged openness between them. This did not meet initially with their expectations of the helper and the implicit contract in which they saw the third party giving advice and instruction. However, they began to see that this was not necessary as feedback enabled them to 'bring themselves into line' spontaneously. So they were learning through a heightened sense of awareness rather than through following rules or instructions.

Eighteen months after the start of these meetings and nine months after the researcher had arrived, there was a change in branch manager. This completely altered the situation. The researcher was joined by the OD manager and they worked as a team. The strategy would have to be revised. The relationship between management and union would have to be built up all over again. The syndicate would probably continue but it would be affected by the need to re-establish trust and understanding. Though encouraged to carry on the syndicate, by senior management, the new branch manager might not want to conduct his relations with the union in the same way and might see future developments going in a new direction. He was after all, inheriting a venture that was not his own. This meant that objectives would have to be reviewed and agreed with the union if commitment was to continue.

To help, the consultant and researcher outlined with the outgoing branch manager the kind of characteristics needed by his successor as a guide to those selecting him. They sought to ease his induction by asking the syndicate to consider what he might be experiencing and to choose a task he could join in easily. They counselled the branch manager and union convenor individually throughout the first few months on issues, attitudes, negotiations, roles and structures. They continued attending syndicate meetings to help the branch manager and the syndicate get to know each other and learn how to work together, to facilitate communication and help clarify objectives and procedure during meetings. All these were powerful methods of learning, based on the principles of dealing with issues as they occur and covering all aspects of experience—tasks and relationships, behaviour and structure. In fact the branch manager picked up the idea of reviewing meetings and relations. He called a meeting with union officials to review a series of nitty-gritty negotiations on the implementation of the technological change and to discuss the sources of mistrust that had built up in their relationship. The researcher was invited to attend to facilitate communication. These methods of learning and building relationships were already becoming part of the ongoing life of the place.

Over the next few months the syndicate went through some difficult patches, and at one meeting the idea of joint syndicate training was discussed after the identification of some clear symptoms of ineffectiveness (poor achievement, the tendency to get cut off from the workforce, ineffective meetings). The researcher and OD manager set out objectives in relation to these needs: agenda setting (criteria and process); the dynamics and stages of problem solving; group member skills; and strategies for involving the workforce. These were presented to the syndicate, who accepted them but never actively owned them. The branch manager and some shop stewards and foremen were keen on the training but expected to be told what they needed rather than encouraged to find out. This may have been overcome if the trainers had followed the principle of the collaborative contract completely by asking them to set the training objectives. But the trainers hoped that as the training progressed the syndicate would take it over and direct it themselves.

There were four training sessions in all, at fortnightly intervals. They were held in syndicate in the room in which they met normally, and in the morning before their usual meeting in the afternoon. So the training was very much in the real-life context and any learning could be immediately put into effect in the afternoon, completing the learning process. The method used was to feedback passages from tapes of previous meetings relevant to learning objectives. The trainer would stop the tape and ask questions either about the content of what was said (listening exercise) or the behaviour at the meeting (perception and feedback). Sometimes other data would be used (records of task progress; results of a post-meeting questionnaire on the topic and meeting). Using this direct feedback on themselves as the basic method enabled them to deepen their understanding of themselves and each other, and learn what to do about it. They were encouraged to raise their own questions, assess themselves and direct their own learning. The training was, through the feedback, closely related to real issues.

The feedback and discussion that followed the playback of tapes covered roles, procedures, concepts and skills on the one hand, and the feelings, attitudes and dynamics of their relations on the other. In the first session the syndicate looked at task-related skills (factors governing choice of agenda, such as source, time, authority) and their behaviour (the stages and process of decision making) The second session looked at task-related skills in the early stages of problem solving (getting and recording information, raising questions to direct diagnosis) some social skills (asking questions, re-stating) and, above all, the emotions and dynamics that made it difficult to agree on the problem or its causes (trust, differences in criteria and objectives, intensity of feelings etc). This last area was crucial as the management conducted problem solving as if it was a purely rational process. The third session focused on the impasse reached in making and evaluating a proposal, and as such was all about the dynamics of the relationship between the personalities of the union and management leaders. Difficulties in expressing reservations by the one leading to suspicion, over-commitment and the forcing of a proposal by the other were examined. The fourth session on negotiating, covered behaviour (stages of negotiating), norms (should there be negotiation and the 'wearing of hats' in the syndicate?) and dynamics (management sitting and listening and drawing the union out, interpretation of agreements). These training sessions considered the 'whole man', the feelings behind behaviour as well as the skills and concepts to carry it out. There could be no change unless there was a change in the relationship and therefore, with both parties in the room together, great emphasis was laid on developing each's understanding of the other. This would not have been possible if learning had not taken place within the on-going relationship.

The actual results of the training bear all this out. There were many insights and observations but little change in behaviour, as the will to change behaviour was connected with the relationship and their feelings about each other. Observations were either based on instruction and concepts introduced by the trainers, or they were spontaneous, on playback of the tape, with session 2 producing the most animated discussion (on questioning motives, intensity of emotion, jumping to conclusions, closed minds, etc) and raising the level of sensitivity. The branch manager alone showed behaviour change, asking more questions, restating, consensus testing. No one was listening during a heated meeting following the second session except the branch manager who was incessantly pointing this out. In the last session the trainer used this as an example of how learning is not put into practice unless feelings are considered as well as perception and behaviour. Although they knew they were not listening they did not do so because they did not want to and because of their strength of feeling. This went down well with foremen and stewards, who said, 'You can't listen or see what is going on if you are emotionally involved'. All along their view of training was to be given a procedure, new set of habits or formula to follow to counteract their usual tendencies. By the end they had begun to see there was more to learning and there were other ways of making changes.

The training had focused on skills and conditions for cooperation, in line with the overall strategy which had emphasized this rather than conflict-handling. However, despite the training, day to day relations had deteriorated to such an extent that training was virtually impossible, with the union complaining that management was using problem solving to their own advantage. The time had come to look at the conflict-handling side of the relationship, and establish trust through building a strong bargaining relationship rather than by cooperative problem solving. This was why the last training session focused on negotiating rather than problem solving. But things had come to such a head that the union would hardly sit round the table with management. Management was being accused of acting without talking, putting everything into dispute, breaking agreements, and taking away foremen's authority. This could all be traced back to the new branch manager's need to learn the ropes, not knowing or trusting his foremen, being dependent on his seniors, using the procedure protectively and having a different view of management's prerogative. The trainers asked the syndicate to separate into management and union groups for each side to set out on paper its perceptions of each other. They then came together to exchange and explore the reasons behind these views and so identify problem areas. This reduced tension but did not result in much action as they tackled the problem of 'communications' by drawing up a formal chart of responsibilities. The union did not want to carry on releasing tension as it might let management 'off the hook' and not lead to any action. However, further progress was made through individual counselling with the branch manager, and later through each side setting out on paper its needs and objectives for improving the industrial relations. The branch manager's were to explore differences in values and criteria, build trust, establish a norm of robust conflict, and create new structures for involvement in decision making. The union convenor's were to have consultation before action and to tackle problems created by breach of agreements, lack of involvement, autocracy and militancy, frustration, over-eagerness and insecurity, The two parties had therefore already reached a greater understanding of each other's needs and expectations and values. Moreover, by the trainers tackling the crisis in this way both sides were learning how they could manage and develop their relationship differently. The training was focusing on real issues in the relationship directly.

The branch manager had initiated two projects for the syndicate, job enrichment and industrial democracy. A non-partisan agency (the Department of Employment Work Research Unit) was called in to talk about job enrichment. The stewards were supplied with information from the TUC on industrial democracy. The researcher worked with the stewards as a group helping them to clarify their fears and objectives. This empowered the union side to think and ask questions about decision making and all the issues around industrial democracy. The convenor wrote a paper for the Bullock Committee. The stewards even asked for a report of their meeting to be shown to management. This gave management a more accurate picture of the stewards and greatly improved the relationship. This again was developing new skills and knowledge, building a more effective balance of power, and increasing mutual understanding by working on real issues with the parties involved. In summary it is possible to say that the results of this experience were that: after the first year, the weekly meeting itself, rather than any direct training or feedback, had changed the way problems were tackled in departments and increased the understanding between management and union. Relations between foremen and stewards were better. There were not fewer disputes but they were tackled differently through trying to reach the causes. In the second year, the syndicate had been useful for both sides to talk through their difficulties. The new branch manager had picked up the changes started by his predecessor and introduced a new direction. The stewards had learnt about industrial democracy and what changes in structure they wanted. Above all both sides had learnt more about how to build the kind of industrial relations they wanted by exchanging expectations and objectives and by reviewing negotiations and their relations.

CONCLUSION

Through these two examples we have attempted to show some of the principles behind the developmental approach in action. The first illustrated the benefits to be derived from a fully collaborative contract with all parties concerned so that management was more responsible for, and involved in their training. The second has shown the need to attend to the ongoing relationship and to produce learning through working on this, with all parties present. This stressed the importance of considering feelings behind behaviour, not just skills and concepts, which means keeping the whole man in mind. The value of keeping close to the real issues and problems was also a lesson from this experience.

D *JOB REDESIGN*

Eric Mitchell

Redesigning jobs is one way of increasing both organizational effectiveness and the satisfaction that employees gain from their working lives. Many people also believe it to be a good way of introducing greater worker participation either as an alternative or as a complement to worker directors, extension of collective bargaining and so on. Although job redesign is by no means a panacea for all organizational ills, its versatility and its potential for completely transforming the way people work together make it a tool that a growing number of enterprises are using.

The author selects job redesign as a most valuable means of developing an organization from a classification of seven ways in which change can be affected. The factors which need to be examined in redesigning jobs are described and attention is drawn to some of the broader implications of an OD intervention based on job redesign. Eric Mitchell also outlines the role of the personnel function in job redesign and makes a case for the personnel specialist to play a major part in initiating and running job redesign programmes.

THE CASE FOR JOB REDESIGN

A case for job redesign as an organization development approach to improve both organizational effectiveness and employees' job satisfaction at work may be made on a number of counts.

First, so far as the individual is concerned, his job not only occupies his time while earning money to live, it is a means of meeting his personal needs such as those for identification and status. The job demands and the way in which work is organized also to a great extent define the possible social contacts at work. Few jobs are so well organized that personal frustrations do not occur, or that improvements cannot be made to match better the technical demands of the job with the personal expectations and abilities of the job holder.

Secondly, it is important for organizational effectiveness to use people's ability to the full, to take account of their needs and to provide the opportunity for people to develop their skills. Designing jobs to do this makes people feel that the company is concerned about them and helps them to become more committed to the organization and its problems. As a result they may become

95

more flexible in their attitudes and help the organization adapt to pressures applied to it from the outside environment. This is what a company needs in the turbulent conditions of the present, when changes are following upon each other thick and fast. Only by adaptation can the organization remain effective and so continue to contribute to the social and economic health of the country.

Thirdly in the present political and social climate the way in which decisions are made is changing. There is a movement towards more participation and industrial democracy. Job redesign requires the participation of job holders for how else can their frustrations needs and ideas be expressed? It is possible therefore to use job redesign to develop participation. Only in a very few cases do people avoid the opportunity of participating in job redesign.

Fourthly, people generally find it easier to be drawn into discussions about their jobs than into discussions about their behaviour at work. Discussions about behaviour often feel threatening because people are not always able or willing to discuss their feelings 'in public'. Also, behaviour is a subject that is found by most people to be an abstract concept whereas their job is something concrete that they can describe. However, having started discussions on jobs and their organization, it is possible to raise behaviour in a less threatening way. It is possible to discuss the relationships and the behaviour between people whose work brings them into contact, for example the sales and the progress clerks or the production operator and the maintenance fitter. Furthermore it is possible at an appropriate moment, in a project group discussion about a job, to stop the meeting and comment on the behaviour of that group at that meeting. This calls for the use of a person who has been trained in group dynamics or in process consultancy. This type of intervention raises issues such as the constraints upon effective group working, and how improvement in the behavioural skills of the individuals and of the group can be made.

WAYS OF PRODUCING ORGANIZATIONAL CHANGE

Katz and Kahn[53] point out that there are seven ways in which organizational change can be effected:

1 Providing information. The supplying of information has a real but limited value as a way of creating organizational change. It is not often a source of motivational force for change but a support to other methods of change.
2 Individual counselling, in which a person is helped with his own personal problems, leaves the individual to translate his new personal insights into organizational change.
3 Peer group influence. Peers do have a strong influence on individual behaviour, and the process of change successfully initiated in a peer group may become self-energizing and self-reinforcing. However, if the peer group

consists of strangers without a common organizational affiliation, they are left as individuals to effect changes on the organization. If the peer group is a work group from an organization, it is likely to be inhibited in its change efforts by the role and authority structure which characterizes it in the organizational setting. Thus only if the whole organization goes through a carefully planned group process will it be affected.

4 Individual sensitivity training. Making individuals sensitive to their own personal strengths and weaknesses leaves them with a problem of adapting their own individual learning into the organizational context. Sensitivity training on its own is not sufficient to produce organizational change.

5 Group dynamics training. Significant results have been shown by, for example, both the Tavistock group process[54] courses and the 'managerial grid'.[55] Few organizations have gone through all the phases of the grid or used the Tavistock group process courses in an organized or programmatic way in which all employees have been involved.

6 Survey feedback. A well organized procedure in which relevant findings are discussed by each working group with their boss, perhaps in a 'cascade' process from the top of the organization down. The target of this demonstrably effective technique are the personal and role relationships within the organizational family. It is one of the more powerful processes for obtaining change in organizations and is often used in the diagnosis step of job redesign programmes.

7 Structural change. This can be the most effective approach to organizational change because it can cause different behaviour patterns. Different behaviours can effect a change in attitudes, which in turn reinforce the structural alterations. Job redesign is a structural approach in which factors or variables in the work situation are altered. Provided the effects are not deliberately confined to a small group or department they will ripple out and cause changes in other areas and systems as described later in a review of some of the implications of this approach. Job redesign planned on a broad basis will cause organizational changes as the roles, objectives, and responsibilities of departments or functions of the business are challenged.

In practice companies tend to begin job redesign programmes for a variety of reasons. At one extreme they may seek to redesign jobs because they have problems such as high labour turnover, high absenteeism, high accident rate or other indicators of frustration and alienation. These problems are often seen as being caused by dissatisfaction with work, and often lead to 'poor industrial relations' or an inability or unpreparedness to make changes. In one company for example, the latter showed itself in the maintenance area by a refusal to agree to changes in the fitters' and the mates' jobs, even though both of the jobs would have been upgraded as a result.

At the other extreme they may make changes as a positive action to maintain or improve the company's standing as good employers with above average conditions of employment and a participative management style. Some companies are looking at ways of improving procedures or conditions of employment, for example developing staff conditions, single status, or harmonizing conditions between hourly, weekly and monthly staff. Other companies have been exploring the provision of information, which in fact is one of the least effective ways of producing organizational change. Yet other companies have been trying to develop more participative practices at work. In one company participation became an end in itself, with a desperate search for something to participate about. Some experience has shown that there is no better vehicle for the development of participation in an organization than through job redesign, with all job holders in turn being offered the opportunity to discuss their jobs with their union representatives and bosses. Discussions about altering procedures and conditions of employment in the organization often quickly run into negotiating barriers, and it is usually preferable to tackle job redesign before going into the revision of procedures and conditions. The process of job redesign should improve the level of trust and improve the skills of working together on problems so that the later discussions on procedures and conditions can go ahead more efficiently.

The personnel specialist is most often the person who makes out the case for a job redesign programme. In general the line manager is under great pressure for day to day results and his reward system is not so concerned with the longer term consequences of his actions. Their personnel function often takes on a concern for the development of a better atmosphere or a more participative style in order to improve effectiveness. However, as advisers, it is not easy for most personnel people to persuade the line managers to risk short term results for long term gains, especially when the precise results are difficult to define, quantify or to guarantee in advance, and when in effect there is an implied element of criticism of the present. Thus it is possible to find many cases where the personnel function is keen to initiate a job redesign programme , but is unable to persuade line management to act. Many diagnoses and attitude surveys have been carried out and reports written with no further action taking place. Many of these have in effect been carried out in order (usually unconsciously) to avoid action and yet to reassure everyone that something is being done. It is vital at the outset to develop some commitment and some understanding about the aims and the wider implications of good job redesign programmes and to plan the process carefully. The personnel manager can often take on the expert educational role in order to obtain wide understanding and commitment, but he should also take on a wider role of acting as a process consultant to plan the process and to help with the development of participation.

What do we mean by job redesign?

In order to define what is meant by job redesign in practice, rather than produce extracts from the voluminous theoretical writings on the subject, the factors or variables related to the job which can often be changed are listed with some brief examples and results. But first two general points need to be made about the OD approach to job redesign.

First, a new form of work design is not a structure for all time. It is often one step taken by an organization on a long road of adjustment to meet better the present technical economic, political and social demands of the environment, and the present job holders' abilities, expectations and needs. Some of these demands and expectations will inevitably change with the passage of time and so make further adjustment necessary. There is therefore a need for flexible attitudes to be developed together with an understanding that, in order to survive, both the organization and the individual must adapt, and that change is an inevitable and permanent part of life. Species of pre-historic animals that did not, or could not, adapt to changes in the environment died out. Healthy job redesign programmes develop people through involving them in the diagnosis, planning and evaluation of the programme of change, and so develop their understanding of the pressures of the outside world and increase their ability to cope with uncertainty and change on a continuing basis.

Secondly, there is no set of rules applicable to every situation. In every case careful analysis needs to be undergone to find out which factors are relevant and what constraints and opportunities for change exist. Furthermore, the possibilities for redesign must be developed from the work and organization demands and employees' expectations, frustrations, needs and abilities in a particular work group. This requires the participation of the job holders. It is not possible to transfer job designs from one work group to another, *en bloc*.

The work methods or tasks demanded by the process, product or technology are one of the first areas which require examination for factors which can be changed. The tools, equipment, raw materials, in-process materials, product and process used should be challenged for what might be called 'method study' improvements. In almost every case it is possible to question some part of the technical design which has a direct bearing on the job demands and job holders' frustrations at work. For example, can the four old furnaces, which keep breaking down, be replaced by two new furnaces placed nearer to the casting machine? Or can a method be devised to remove the need for one girl to spend all her time scraping the finished product off an endless belt? Is the product specification too tight? In one example the tightness of in-process material specifications were found to be caused not by customer demands but by the way in which assembly had been organized, and a different assembly process removed the need for this tight specification and eliminated one very boring task. So often, it is found, operators put up with inefficiencies in the method because they have given up asking management who 'cannot afford capital expenditure to make improvements' but who in fact have been losing money for years through not listening and making improvements to the methods. The assumptions that the arrangement of the technical aspects of the task are immutable requires questioning.

The relationship between the technical demands or tasks and the jobs as they are now organized is a second area to be looked at to find other ways in which jobs and tasks may be matched. Many jobs consist of fragments of a whole task and may appear meaningless to the job holders. A more meaningful task for most people is one where the job holder sees the beginning and the end of some significant part of the process. For example, a meaningful task can include the preparation doing and evaluation of a whole task. In this way a variety of skills can be built into the job, and the job holder may feel he is doing a job which is of some significance and with which he can identify. For example, the assembly and the final testing of an electric fire can be a more meaningful task for some people (but not for everyone) than say merely fitting one part onto the fire in an assembly line. In another case, preparing the mould, moulding, knocking out the products, and removing the burrs is a more meaningful whole task for some people. It is often possible to find other options if the whole process of production of the product is mapped out together with the activities of any support or service groups. In this way the logic may be shown of pulling into a job simple planning, inspecting or maintenance activities or of forming semi-autonomous groups where the whole task is shared between a number of people.

This leads into the third area which is concerned with the *information flows* required to carry out tasks. In order to carry out a task efficiently the job holder needs to know not only what to do, and how to do it, but he may also need to know the sequence in which orders should be tackled. Provision of information of this type to the person who should be in control of the job (ie the job holder) can enlarge the job and increase both job satisfaction and effectiveness. Sometimes it is necessary to draw charts of who receives information and who needs the information to do the tasks quickly and efficiently. This can enable the job holders to take on, for example, short-term planning. Planning the short-term sequence in which orders are processed can increase both efficiency and satisfaction in situations where the operator can respond to complex differing demands such as, for example, these experienced in colour mixing. Given orders for a day's work, a competent colour mixer can from experience put his orders in sequence in a way which minimizes the number of times he has to clean down his mixing equipment that day. This can increase output, reduce contamination problems, increase job satisfaction and produce a much better outcome than where a progress planner, who has never done the job, plans the sequence on a theoretical basis. The possibility of changing the flow of information to allow the job holder to carry out some planning is thus a factor for consideration in job redesign.

Extending the amount of information available to the job holder to include that concerned with the quantity or quality of output can enable him to evaluate his own performance. It may also enable him, if appropriately trained, to take corrective action if the product process or service goes out of specification. This assumes that he has control over the output, which is not always true. For example, in one job redesign programme tests were developed which for the first time enabled the operator to know whether the final product was going to be within or without the specification, and enabled him to take action to bring it back within the limits if it was failing the test.

In order to take corrective actions it is necessary not only to have the relevant information but also to make decisions. This is the fourth area of factors which can be changed in job redesign—*decision making*. In most work situations it is possible to list the decisions which have to be made during normal operation and when things go wrong (eg when the automatic process has to be run manually or when the product quality is out of specification). These two lists of decisions can be examined to see who is best to take them, using criteria of organizational effectiveness and satisfaction of the job holders. It may be necessary to give additional training to help people acquire the requisite skills to make the decisions and to take the necessary actions. Taking on more decision making is a powerful way in which people can have more responsibility. Through the exercise of more judgement and discretion they can experience more autonomy in their work, and can usually increase the speed of response to out of the ordinary events and thus increase organizational effectiveness.

An examination of decision making responsibilities naturally leads on to the fifth area of factors which can be changed in job design and which is concerned with *organizational design*. In order to achieve organization objectives certain activities have to be carried out and these require the use of resources. In all but the smallest firms specialist departments are set up to support the line departments to achieve the business objectives. All the line and staff departments have objectives, are accountable for certain activities and have authority over certain resources. The existence, roles and responsibilities of all of these departments should be examined so that all the different ways in which effective and meaningful jobs can be built up are considered. In making decisions about departments and their responsibilities, due emphasis should be placed upon building up jobs which contain planning, doing and evaluating tasks with the necessary information and discretion to make decisions.

Managerial positions are required within the departments to provide the employees with support and expertise. A hierarchical structure is best developed in practice from an examination of the requirements of both the top and the bottom of the organization. There are often clear-cut legal or functional requirements for certain top positions (eg finance, marketing, research and development). In order to maintain the competence of some specialist departments it is necessary to have departmental heads concerned not only with meeting today's objectives but also with developing the expertise of the function and its contribution to the business in the long term. At the bottom of the organization it is possible to define work groups which have similar objectives, share the same whole task, are engaged in making the same product or are geographically related etc. These groups may require an internal leader to provide the group with internal support (eg a person to whom members can turn when they cannot solve their own internal problems). In addition the group may require support and assistance with problems external to the group (ie between the group and other groups, or between the groups and the outside environment) and this may require the establishment of managerial positions with the responsibility to manage the group boundaries. By examining such organizational and work group requirements, the different ways in which a hierarchy of management roles may be designed can be put forward and evaluated, using criteria of organizational effectiveness and job satisfaction. The status or grade of these positions has to be found by job evaluation.

In many job redesign studies an examination of the organization aspects leads to a reduction in the number of levels in the hierarchy, or a reduction in the number of managers. This point is discussed further in the section on implications. However, as a result of an examination of these organizational aspects, people should have a clearer understanding of their own role and the responsibilities of their departments. In order to avoid confusion these concepts need to be shared and agreed upon with peers, subordinates and superiors.

THE BROADER IMPLICATIONS OF AN ORGANIZATION DEVELOPMENT INTERVENTION BASED ON JOB REDESIGN

An OD approach, using job redesign as a vehicle, can enable the behavioural aspects of organizational life to be improved, direct participation to develop and decision making to be pushed down in the organization. All of which is a step towards increasing democracy at the workplace. If jobs are changed, with the participation of the job holders, it is likely that they will learn new skills and will personally develop and begin to expect more from work. Thus many systems for which the personnel function are responsible may be challenged. Are the works rules compatible with the enriched jobs and with the employees' more responsible attitudes? The job descriptions will need rewriting and the jobs re-evaluating. In two large UK companies it has been found necessary to redesign the job evaluation scheme because it could not cope satisfactorily with the increased mental and social skills demanded by the redesigned jobs. Are the present incentive schemes still appropriate? Can new incentive schemes be devised to meet both organization and individual employee needs? Is a group incentive scheme more appropriate? Should payment based on the scheme be made weekly, monthly or quarterly or even yearly? Is a multi-factor scheme appropriate based on, say, raw material or machine utilization, together with output and perhaps other broad parameters? Finally, is the salary structure appropriate now? As a consequence of the changes is there reason to question the number of payment grades and the differentials between grades in the salary structure? If there is a band of payment appropriate to each grade how should personal movement in the band be decided (by what criteria and by what process)?

Conditions of employment may be challenged, especially in the design of semi-autonomous work groups. If people in the same work group have different conditions of employment, are they appropriate under the new circumstances? Can the differences be justified and are they felt to be reasonable and fair? In a factory producing metal products the operation required a technician to carry out X-ray analysis of the molten metal before it could be used. It was necessary therefore for the X-ray technicians to work the same hours as the operators in the group. In the group discussions about ways in which the jobs could be redesigned it became clear that much of the warfare that went on between the X-ray technicians and the operators was due to the different conditions of employment that existed and which were very favourably biased towards the technicians, who were on staff. They worked a different shift system, had different overtime allowances and holiday entitlements and so on, all of which worked to the advantage of the technicians. So that although the operators and X-ray technicians were drawn together by the technical demands of the job, because of the technicians' staff status with its better conditions, they were alienated from the operators; this caused big relationship problems that reduced organizational efficiency. It is therefore necessary to look out for differences in employment conditions between the members of work groups, and to consider the case for 'harmonizing' them or moving towards single status conditions. Harmonizing conditions of employment is well advanced in some companies and countries (for example, the French mensualization programme).

The personnel procedures may also require to be adapted as a consequence of a job redesign programme. Are the procedures compatible with the new jobs and the new attitudes? If the jobs have changed, possibly it is necessary to recruit people with different skills and perhaps to amend the selection process. If highly integrated group working is developed, should not the final steps in selection be undertaken by group members? Do the training and induction processes need altering? Are the appraisal procedures compatible with the new jobs, organizational structure and attitudes? How will career development be handled in the future? What is the promotion selection procedure and is it still appropriate? Do the grievance and dispute handling procedures need alteration?

The final point in this section is on manning which is, of course, a matter of considerable significance to the personnel function. It can emerge as an issue in job redesign projects where an increase in overall efficiency has not been matched by an increase in the order book. Indeed a 'no enforced redundancy' clause is a not uncommon feature of job redesign projects. What is crucial is that, at the outset of the project, the implications for manning should be discussed and if necessary a way of resolving expected problems should be agreed.

The case for the personnel function to initiate and act as consultant in job redesign programmes

For the present purpose the personnel function can be considered to be concerned with providing three things: an effective organization; appropriate people; and optimal employment conditions. These three are closely inter-related and changes in one can affect the other two. If jobs are redesigned to make the organization more effective, different skills and therefore different people may be required. Also experience of job redesign programmes in firms shows that job changes tend to raise employees expectations and they may demand employment conditions which they feel are more compatible with the new jobs. In addition, job redesign can result in changes in personnel procedures (eg selection, induction, training etc) and system (eg job evaluation, incentives, salary structure etc). Hence it is essential that the personnel function is closely involved in job redesign programmes.

Furthermore, job redesign is concerned with producing a better fit between the organization's technical demands and the social needs of the employees. The personnel function is concerned with these human needs. It is suggested that it ought to be concerned with the process of change which leads to a better match between the technical and the social needs, and with the integration of the structural design approach with the behavioural aspects for which it is already usually responsible (eg industrial relations, procedures of conflict resolution, and personnel selection development and training etc).

The process of change can in fact, for these purposes, be considered to consist of three steps: developing awareness; planning and carrying out change; and evaluating the results of change.

The personnel function can play a big part in developing an awareness of the benefits of a job redesign approach. Because of its contact with the environment and through its concern with industrial relations and legislation in the personnel field, it should itself be aware of the political and social trends outside the organization. It needs to transfer this awareness to the line and specialist departments for the benefit of both these departments and the organization. This awareness needs to be developed not only in the minds of those who are concerned with the day to day running of the organization but also in the minds of those who are designing new products, processes, machines or factories for the future. There is a need to make sure that everyone, chemist, accountant, engineer and in fact all the specialists, become more concerned about the quality of life at work of all employees and about ways in which it can be improved.

The personnel function should also act as a process consultant to help the people involved to go more effectively through the process of job redesign or development of any kind. They will not generally be qualified to make unilateral decisions about the content of jobs, people's needs and abilities, or the technical aspects of the process or product, but they should be able to help the departments, functions, groups and individuals to collaborate together to find the different options available and to assist them in making decisions about which design is best. Most personnel people will require training in these skills.

Finally, the personnel function should take on the role of evaluating the effect of these changes and of helping the organization to continuously adapt to the pressures applied to it. In this way personnel specialists can help the organization and the individuals in it to remain healthy.

In many of the more sophisticated (and usually larger) companies the personnel function is already taking on this role. In a very few companies it has been doing this for 10 years or more. A detailed discussion of how to carry out a job redesign programme is not the subject of this paper. However, the following five important points should be borne in mind in using an OD approach to job redesign:

1 It is necessary for top management and union support and understanding to be obtained, especially of the implications of a job redesign programme.
2 It is essential that all the managers, unions and employees involved or affected by a project should be kept fully informed, and should be given the opportunity to contribute to the analysis, planning and implementation of change.
3 The approach should be initially from the bottom up, working with volunteer job holders to analyse and redesign their working situation. Change should then ripple up into the systems, procedures and other organizational aspects. The pervasiveness of this ripple effect is bound to be influenced by

the effectiveness of the communication and consultation processes throughout the company.

4 There is a need for someone to be made responsible for the job redesign programme and to act as consultant to the individuals and groups. He will require special skills and training is vital.

5 The programme depends upon trust and upon people learning and growing. This takes time and job redesign should be recognized as being about developing new attitudes, new styles of management involving the creation of improved information flows and greater openness.

CHAPTER V

Case Studies in OD

A   An organization-wide approach to industrial relations training in the Health Service
Graham Smith

B   The role of the personnel specialist in changing management development in a manufacturing company
Dean Wilson

C   Establishing a permanent OD role in the personnel function of BAT (UK and Export) Ltd
Jeremy Ridge

D   Team introduction workshops: a method of speeding up the integration of new team members
Roger Plant

A   *In the first case study, **Graham Smith** clarifies the critical differences between the conventional and the OD approach to training. He then sets out in detail how, in response to a request for training in industrial relations and negotiating skills, the personnel and training specialists helped the management of a district in the Health Service to build a policy and a strategy for improving industrial and employee relations. The author shows how the principles behind the OD approach, similar to those outlined in John Bristow and Rod Scarth's paper, were successfully put into action at each stage of the project. He also describes the role taken by the personnel and training specialists and the kind of skill they needed. This further illustrates some of the points raised by Brian Wilson in chapter 2.*

B   *In the second of the case studies, **Dean Wilson** brings out the dual role of the personnel manager as a technical expert and as a manager of change. This is one of the central themes of his paper. He sees the personnel manager as managing (as distinct from facilitating) change when it is within his* *own function but, like Brian Wilson, shows how he can use OD technology to help in this. He draws up the elements and the outline of a change strategy, identifying goals, building up need, vision and commitment. Dean Wilson neatly describes how the goals of an OD project in management development cover all aspects of the functioning of an organization (policies, relationships, structures, systems and individual skills) with each aspect balancing and following the other in sequence. This distinguishes it from a conventional approach which might seek to change procedures and skills only. On the technical side, his examples of management development policies, strategies and activities are instructive, and can be fruitfully read in conjunction with the paper on appraisal in the previous chapter.*

C   *In the third case study **Jeremy Ridge** describes how a permanent OD role was established in the personnel function of BAT (UK and Export). He tells of how past experience of OD through Grid and MBO programmes and a state of confusion over direction led to the formation of the role. In defining it he stresses the need to combine a business orientation with behavioural science skills, and to be concerned with the company organization as a whole as well as the functions of personnel. The author points out how it was necessary for the emergent OD role to fit into the existing culture, talk the managers' 'own' language, and generally establish credibility by helping with specific current problems. Once established, OD assisted corporate planning in cross-functional teams and helped the board through a team development programme. This case study shows the kind of role in OD that the personnel function can play, especially where it is well established and where organizing requires considerable understanding and competence.*

D   *Finally, **Roger Plant**, describes his experiences as an internal consultant in helping management teams to minimize the disruption caused by changes in team membership. His case study centres around the work done in helping a new managing director to integrate quickly and effectively into a senior management team. This activity was jointly focused on the needs of the newcomer and those of the other members of the team. The techniques used by Roger Plant simply and clearly illustrate OD in action and the data which emerged from the team introduction workshop (summarized at the end of the paper) together with the results of evaluation of the workshop, show the extent and variety of outcomes possible from this kind of exercise.*

Case study A

AN ORGANIZATION-WIDE APPROACH TO INDUSTRIAL RELATIONS TRAINING IN THE HEALTH SERVICE

INTRODUCTION

This study describes an OD project within the National Health Service, currently being undertaken in Portsmouth and South East Hampshire Health District.* Its major objective is to develop the relationships between employees in the organization.

Portsmouth Health District serves a population of 527,000 people contained in 320 square miles. It has a workforce of 7000, comprising five major disciplines: nursing (3400); administration, clerical and engineering (750); scientific/technical (550); ancillary (2200) and medical (220 hospital staff plus 230 GPs). Portsmouth District is the largest of four Health Districts making up Hampshire Area Health Authority, which itself is part of the Wessex Regional Health Authority. However, for the purpose of this study the District should be regarded as autonomous.

OD VERSUS TRAINING

Organization development is not a unique discipline in itself but rather an approach to problems which we all can take, including training officers. OD is characterized, and differentiated from traditional training methods, by a set of principles which will be emphasized during the course of this study. However, it is appropriate that some of the fundamental distinctions between the two approaches should be drawn right from the start—as a guide to the beliefs and assumptions of the author.

Traditional training programmes essentially centre on individuals, and on fitting them, through the provision of specific skills and knowledge, to prescribed roles in their organization. Such training is commissioned, and the objectives set, by senior management or trainers but is applied to employees in lower levels of the company's hierarchy. The trainer maintains this culture

* The author recognizes with gratitude the permission given by the Management of the District to reproduce much of the material contained in this study

through being directive and expository in the training events. The basic assumption is that the overall effectiveness of an organization can be increased by *improving* the performance of individual employees within prescribed limits.

OD focuses on the total organization, seeking to improve its efficacy, and individuals' satisfaction, through changing the relationships between various factors in the organization's situation. These factors include the objectives and structure of the enterprise; its culture; the roles of, and relationships between, employees; attitudes and behaviour; and the outcomes of the organization in human and physical terms. *Development* is achieved through progress to a defined future state. The OD approach is top management led, but involves all employees who will be affected by organization change in the setting of change objectives. OD facilitators maintain this theme through action research programmes and experiential learning activities. It emphasizes that the organization's employees must believe in the necessity for change, and take over the implementation of action-plans. OD also attempts to validate individuals within the context of what is usually a continuing, or long-term, process.

The two descriptions should be seen as statements about the central values of each method, not as opposing poles or a positive/negative judgement. This case study will include elements of both, although the underlying philosophy is that of OD. Several phases are discernible in the study, the major ones being contract building; diagnosis and action planning; implementation; monitoring; and review. Before describing the first stage of the project some background material is required.

THE CLIENTS AND THEIR ORGANIZATION

Health Districts are managed by a six-person team: a district administrator (DA); district nursing officer (DNO); district finance officer (DFO); district community physician (DCP); representative consultant and general practitioner members. The task of the district management team (DMT), as well as formulating planning proposals for district services and co-ordinating their implementation, is to 'take decisions jointly on matters which are not exclusively the responsibility of any one of them and which are not provided for in approved plans nor regulated by established policies of the area health authority'.[56]

The DMT comprises both managers and representatives, the DA being responsible for four administrative sectors employing staff at 23 hospitals or homes (three containing over 600 beds) and 105 clinics and health centres. The DNO is accountable for six nursing divisions staffing these sites, and the DFO controls a yearly pay bill of over £18½ million as well as capital monies. The district community physician, as well as representing the interests of scientific and technical groups also co-ordinates health care planning teams and preventative health services.

The medical specialities, however, have a representative system and elect a consultant and a GP member to the DMT. These medical representatives protect doctors' interests at all levels as well as participating in decision making for the district. Unlike the top managers on the DMT they have no hierarchical authority over the medical group and cannot be held accountable for the actions of this group.

Before the start of the project the district personnel officer (DPO), who reports directly to the DA, had reviewed the industrial relations scene in Portsmouth district. Items included in his summary were:[57]

trade union and professional associations were growing in size, and in a willingness to use their power

managers and supervisors were unsure of their authority in the industrial relations field, and many issues were being taken directly to senior managers

managers were reacting adversely to the new situation showing suspicion, authoritarianism, abdication, and they had little confidence in using their own initiative

union representatives were trained but managers were not. Staff representatives showed growing impatience with ineffective management responses

communication was poor and inconsistent in the District. Information flowed through union channels much faster than down the management structure

current policies were weakening the line-manager's role and had been developed without their involvement

shop floor power was based on local power groups and their representatives reflected members' views rather than union policies

very little consultation machinery existed

the DMT had had to react, over the preceding 18 months to a number of industrial relations crises whose causes could be categorized as:

    (a)   those concerned with bonus schemes

    (b)   staff welfare, health, or safety

    (c)   frustration at managerial inaction over repeatedly raised grievances.

Most cases in (a) and (b) could have been avoided. The DMT agreed with the personnel officer's conclusion that industrial relations training was required for senior managers. Consequently, the regional personnel division was contacted, and asked to produce a scheme to improve manager's industrial relations skills.

The regional personnel division, which includes an education and training department, is a small unit offering amongst other services specialist advice to Areas and Districts within the Wessex Regional Health Authority on matters of personnel, industrial relations, manpower planning and training. The regional tier of the NHS has no hierarchical relationship with health districts. Two regional officers were to be involved in the Portsmouth project, the regional personnel officer (RPO) and education and training officer (RETO).

Three members of the Portsmouth DMT met the two regional officers to discuss possible training/industrial relations strategies. The DMT were clear about their need for a comprehensive and co-ordinated industrial relations strategy. Their key result areas were:

the negotiation and implementation of consultative machinery
the review and streamlining of management communications
industrial relations training for managers
supporting managers in the application of policies
the surveying and improvement of facilities for staff.

This meeting discussed the issues raised through the DPO's review of industrial relations and highlighted several others: middle managers were also suspicious of top management; different cultures existed on the various hospital sites; nursing managers experienced a severe dilemma between the clinical and managerial demands of their jobs; 'fire-fighting' was the most frequent managerial norm.

A number of factors were already evident:

1 the DMT were highly committed to the development of an industrial relations strategy
2 it was necessary to involve line managers in the development of this strategy
3 the strategy would attack a number of critical factors simultaneously
4 the strategy would be unique to the district; matching the demands of the situation, the tasks to be done and the preferences of management and staff
5 immediate action was required before the current organizational climate deteriorated seriously.

The regional officers suggested that a district industrial relations strategy should have short- and long-term components and recommended the following steps:

For the long term
A meeting of the full DMT, with the DPO and two regional officers, lasting approximately two days, to do the following:

produce a written, long-term, policy document based on the needs of the situation as perceived now for the future

clarify the tasks and responsibilities of the DMT and other senior managers in executing the long- and short-term strategies

if appropriate, clarify the DMT members' roles in handling industrial relations situations

produce a monitoring system so that the DMT can be constantly aware of the pressure points in the district.

For the short term

Three objectives were important:

the need to develop in managers a confidence in their own ability in handling industrial relations issues: a process of *empowerment*

the need for managers to be committed to and understand agreed procedures

the need to identify activities which would quickly improve the industrial relations situation.

A series of multi-disciplinary, three-day workshops were suggested to meet the above, to give managers skills in training subordinates and as a vehicle to build a large cadre of 'trained' managers in a short time.

Relationship between short and long terms

The inputs to the short-term strategy would be based on the DMT's plans for the long term. There would be feedback from the workshops into the long-term plans. The DMT was asked to set aside two/three hours per month to devote to reviewing the short-term outcomes, and to consider more irregular meetings to monitor the continuing viability of the long-term programme.

The DMT agreed to put aside one-and-a-half days of its time to produce a long-term policy, and consider the content for short-term training activities.

Although the DMT's original request for an 'outline for training' could have been construed as commissioning a training programme, it was actually presented with a strategic method. It did not expect to go through this process, but recognized the need to do so. The decision to take the one-and-a-half days to consider the situation sealed the contract between the regional officers and the DMT. This method was accepted because of:

the need to produce an effective organization in the long term, capable of developing and changing itself

the need to change attitudes and improve present managerial competence in industrial relations

the need for a 'critical mass' of managers to be committed to action before any real change would occur such commitment would come through their involvement in the production and implementation of new policies.

The DMT fully realized that, from the moment of defining a long-term approach, industrial relations issues should be tackled in accordance with this approach (portraying the managerial behaviour to be introduced) which would require decisions which might not be the most expedient.

Diagnosis and action planning: December, first year

The six members of the DMT, the DPO, and the two regional officers met at a pastoral retreat some miles from Portsmouth to divorce themselves psychologically from the day to day demands of their jobs. The objectives of the meeting, as stated at the time, were:

- to come to a common understanding of the situation
- to agree the parameters that influence action
- to produce some objectives/philosophies within which the DMT will operate
- to build short- and long-term plans
- to agree a training programme and priorities
- to consider what control mechanisms there are for the industrial relations situation.

To summarize the course of the DMT's retreat:

- the DMT shared a common understanding of the existing state of industrial relations and identified areas of strength and weakness in the district
- an ideal organization culture was then described by identifying criteria by which the DMT could judge the district to have a successful employee relations climate
- the major gaps between what was required and the current situation were established, and alternative ways of closing them discussed
- some of these alternative actions were chosen to be implemented in Portsmouth district
- in some cases the various criteria, or the chosen alternative solutions, were grouped together in clusters where one or two activities might remedy more than one problem, or where several problems seemed to have one root cause
- target dates and responsibilities were assigned
- the process of the one-and-a-half days was reviewed and modifications made to the methods of evaluating the success of activities undertaken.

The day began with a discussion of the external factors influencing industrial

114

relations in the district; focusing down from the national to the local environment. One DMT member suggested considering the situation from both management and trade union viewpoints, and this was adopted to gain some understanding of another major factor in the life of the organization. The technique the DMT and DPO used to describe the various situations was 'brainstorming'—verbalizing their feelings about the industrial relations climate.

This process was facilitated and recorded by the two regional officers. After an intensive morning's work, the two lists contained in figure 1 were produced. In reviewing the situation described in figure 1 the DMT felt itself to have been unduly negative and so it reconsidered the strengths of its current organization, which included the recent establishment of a district joint consultative committee and its own commitment to handling the situation.

Having produced a shared picture of the current scene, the DMT then considered the factors which would characterize the ideal 'healthy' district. The 'brainstorming' technique was again used followed by exhaustive discussion to synthesize and refine the points made. The following statement was produced:

'The way ahead'

1 All major management decisions are arrived at with commitment of all internal parties
2 The 'work group' is committed to its goals through 'local decision making'
3 There are clearly understood goals, which generate commitment
4 There are clearly understood systems and procedures relating to staff
5 Relations between management and staff are such that:
   (a) there is an agreed way of dealing with conflict
   (b) they do not resort to maximum retaliation
   (c) there is trust between individuals and that the 'system' will work
6 Managers and staff representatives have a clearly understood way of solving staff problems
7 Speedy, reliable, sensitive two-way communication
8 Good ideas surface and are acted upon
9 There is an effective representative system
10 There is an ongoing assessment of the industrial relations scene and its consequences.
11 Co-operation between staff and management on how and where people are working
12 Positive approach to Portsmouth district
13 Positive and consistent understanding of roles and authority between AHA, ATO, DMT.

The DMT's next task was to build actions around each of the above criteria

Figure 1 Summary of DMT's subjective analysis of the industrial relations situation in Portsmouth district made during their one day 'retreat'.

A DESCRIPTION OF THE CURRENT DISTRICT SITUATION

(a) From a management perspective

1 Confused
2 Different perspectives
3 Actual authority of DMT
4 Suspicion
5 Authority of DMT
6 Political motives
7 Consultation/participation
8 Climate—chain reaction of external events
9 Freedom of unions—constraints on management
10 TU thrown over moral responsibility
11 Tensions of management
12 Little insight by lower levels of management of DMT
13 Different influence processes between clinicians/line management
14 Direction of DMT
15 Size of 'the group to be influenced'
16 Problem of bureaucracy—industrial relations decision-making *centralized*
17 Updating strategy
18 Apathy apart from 3/4 focal points
19 Getting to rank and file
20 Managers do not use communication system, eg newsletter
21 Are we willing to hold patients to ransom
22 Managers/doctors are 'babes in the wood'
23 There is some goodwill in the district
24 Most of rank and file have not been interested—now their representatives are being challenged if they go too far—(*case* may be exaggerated)
25 Some staff want positive management—leadership
26 Doctors see themselves as key workers—therefore their point must be heard

(b) From a trade union perspective

1 Competition—inter-union/intra-union
2 We want to manage the service/power
3 Past pains, eg no redundancy/no more low pay/staff conditions
4 Management tightening up—firmer more cohesive approach
5 Suspicion of management
6 Little trust
7 Get away with most things
8 Building up membership
9 Stopping management getting to rank and file
10 Prevent management getting a good communication network
11 Full time officials keen to have more controlled approach to industrial relations—controlling their members
12 We are willing to hold patients to ransom to achieve our objectives—management will *always* back down
13 We are well trained and confident of taking on management
14 Our members, though confused, are willing to be led
15 We are a cohesive group
16 Our members are a bit uneasy if we go too far

intended to change the present situation to the agreed desired state. This 'action planning' phase lasted into the second day, when both the content and the style of the management education to be undertaken were considered (to be discussed in the next section).

The 'retreat' saw a number of changes in the assumptions existing at the outset of the project. These transitions are critical to both the progress of the project and in regarding it as an OD activity. The top management group had been involved in defining the problem and developing solutions rather than requesting the personnel specialists to produce a strategy for change. The DMT also resolved to be part of the training events itself, to be heavily involved in the implementation of the action plans and to be accountable for all its actions against published objectives. This differs from many training events where the visible leaders of the activities are training specialists. In this case the client became responsible for the transfer of learning in the 'training' events which were to take place.

Consideration of the causes of present organizational problems had resulted in the project now being aimed at developing employee relations overall, rather than that part called 'industrial relations'. The project now encompassed the culture of the district, not solely the disruptive parts of it. To improve the situation an extensive series of linked activities were planned (see figure 2). This was not simply a training programme as requested at the outset.

The model that the DMT used to produce its action plan was very simple:

1 define current situation
2 identify future or ideal situation
3 plan steps to get from (1) to (2).

This is a very powerful process, as it establishes a direction and set of goals for the organization against which all other organizational objectives can be compared. This method also establishes training goals as part of organizational goals and moves away from pure training objectives (which are usually to do with pictures of ideal managers).

This emphasizes the differences between the technique used during the 'retreat' and traditional course design.

In setting up 'Criteria for a Healthy District' (see figure 2) the DMT was not only fulfilling its role in initiating long-term policy for the district, but was also experiencing a technique to create such policy. The style of managing that the DMT had defined also demanded that all managers (criteria 1 and 3) should have the opportunity to discuss, amend, or drastically change the employee relations philosophy of the district.

The role of the regional officers was twofold. They acted as facilitators in the policy definition process, and as experts in helping towards the design of the management training workshops. These workshops were based on the clients' criteria of organizational health rather than that of the trainers. The trainer sets the questions (as in the three-action plan above) but the client provides the answers. Real organization development is the product of client/facilitator collaboration, rather than the trainer standing apart from the organization.

IMPLEMENTATION: JANUARY/FEBRUARY, YEAR TWO

The DMT's action plans did include three types of training: in induction, the business of the district, and industrial relations skills. These were augmented by the need to introduce managers to the new approach to employee relations and involve them in its development. This was consistent with the open and involving style favoured by the DMT.

It was decided to begin 'training' the key groups of managers at senior and middle levels as soon as possible. About 70 managers from all functions were to be involved.

In discussions with the DMT and a few senior managers, it was agreed that the workshops should follow the pattern of the DMT's 'retreat', in defining the current and required situations and planning to bridge this gap. The content of these training events was drawn from:

1 The history of industrial relations and associated management approaches at a national level, within the NHS and locally in Portsmouth district
2 The DMT's criteria for a healthy district
3 Rules and guidelines on employee relations for managers
4 The role of the manager in creating good employee relations (especially communication and subordinate training)
5 Training in negotiating skills: to build the confidence of managers and in recognition of the demands of the current situation
6 Build a support system—a network of people, literature, sources where managers can go for advice but retain their responsibility
7 Preparation for returning to the organization; recognizing that employees and shop stewards will know that managers have been away and will be looking for changes
8 Planning of further action; identifying omissions from the training, evaluation and up-dating of managers' skills and knowledge.

Although the negotiating skills input was prescribed by top management the bulk of the workshop activities were to be participant-led rather than expository. Three workshops were planned to occur within a space of five weeks

Figure 2 Action plan produced by DMT during 8 December 'retreat'

CRITERIA	ACTION	RESPONSE	DATE
1 All major management decisions arrived at with commitment of all internal parties	1 Review pattern of face to face communication within the district and make suggestions for improvements	DPO/RTO	30 Aug
	2 Implement above		
	3 Formal consultative committees for 'natural groups'	DPO–DCC	31 Jan 30 Apr
	4 Review publicity of DMT minutes		
	5 Item on each DMT agenda 'Matters for DCC'	DA	31 Jan
	6 Education of staff in the 'business of the district'—a programme of activities to take place	DA Consequent upon objectives setting meeting	ASFN
2 The 'work group' is committed to its goals through 'local decision making'	Create in teams (according to management hierarchy) a consultative style by: (a) training activities (b) a systematic build-up of relationship between manager and staff representative		
3 There are clearly understood goals, which generate commitment	1 DMT to set goals for the districts	DMT	31 Mar
	2 Write IR district policy based on these notes for public consumption	DPO and personnel Dept	28 Feb
4 There are clearly understood systems and procedures relating to staff.	Design and agree a procedure for systematically reviewing personnel procedures in the district	DPO	28 Feb
5 Relations between management and staff are such that: (a) there is an agreed way of dealing with conflict (b) do not resort to maximum retaliation (c) there is trust between individuals and that the 'system' will work	1 Train managers in the application of a particular approach to conflict handling negotiating skills		
	2 DMT to produce policy detailing when conflict can be handled locally	DA	10 Jan
6 Managers and staff representatives have a clearly understood way of solving staff problems	Management know areas of authority as in 5 (2) Train management to be more sensitive in recognizing potential areas		
7 Speedy, reliable, sensitive two-way communication	Newcomers to get packet of 'Induction' information Review Criteria 1 (1) with this object Educate management in use of the newsletter	DPO	Easter

in order to build quickly a large group of 'initiated' managers. The two regional officers, the DPO *and* members of the DMT were to act as facilitators during the workshops.

The primary aim of the workshops was:

> to prepare Health Service managers more fully to understand and deal with present and future situations arising from the relationship between employees, their boss, and the organization.[58]

The workshops had three distinct parts, corresponding to each day of the three-day event. The first day was discursive, considering pictures of the present and future district culture and highlighting the issues facing the organization. The second day was concerned with skills development, increasing understanding and improving practice in employee and industrial relations situations. Day three involved action planning for the participants' return to their 'home' organizations, and in amplifying and reinforcing the transfer of learning.

All the DMT attended some part of the workshops and some members of the DMT were present throughout. All presentations of potential policy were given by the DA or DNO, and many other sessions (such as the participants' diagnosis of the local scene) were initiated by DMT members or the DPO. The DMT's involvement and their willingness to rethink what was seen as the first draft of their policy during day one, when the major issues facing the district, including the new objectives, were shared was well received by workshop members and gave confidence to managers in their forthcoming implementation of action plans.

SOME RESULTS

The workshops' programmes were based on real issues in the organization; and this facilitated transfer of the learning to participants. Many of the 70 managers who attended the workshops went back to the workplace and began, either individually or in small groups, to initiate changes. For instance:

> in one sector two managers instituted a series of two-day participative courses to pass on the skills and knowledge they had acquired to middle and first-line managers
>
> a staff handbook was printed
>
> two further staff representative committees were established, with management help, at hospital level
>
> a manual of personnel policies has been produced
>
> more negotiating teams have been established and tested, removing pressure from senior managers.

The DMT itself became more conscious of employee and industrial relations issues and of the effect its own behaviour had on these matters. This gave impetus to following up other action plans from its 'retreat'. On the debit side, it appears that in some parts of the organization the stress and anxiety has gone down one or two levels in the management hierarchy. However, mechanisms had been established to identify and work on this problem.

The workshops provided a cadre of managers to take the principles and commitment to action back to their local organization. This approach succeeded well in some places, but not so well in others, where management practices reverted to custom and habit. Most managers returned to the district prepared to use their own responsibility/authority in attempts to solve outstanding, or novel, employee relations problems. Their activities frequently appeared unco-ordinated, uncontrolled, and not set against any agreed framework except for their understanding of the new district philosophy. The DMT showed considerable insight in not blocking this process of empowerment through reacting to the perceived loss of central control and forcing some sort of order into the proceedings.

The concept of 'critical mass' emphasizes another point. Learning need not only be the process of individuals acquiring knowledge but can and should occur in the social context of the organization. People can learn and change whilst relating to each other in the same ways as they do in the organization, or alternatively they can agree to change values or relate differently to each other. This change is reciprocal, mutual and above all social. In this way people in the organization see the importance of the contribution that each makes and realize that if one factor (a subordinate) changes, then other factors (the superior) *must* change. Organizational change is accomplished through concomitant changes of skills, attitudes, knowledge, relationships and norms, throughout the organization.

MONITORING

The progress of the entire project was watched and evaluated by the DMT and the organization's managers. It soon became evident that the low involvement of medical staff in industrial relations matters, illustrated by their non-attendance at the workshops, was critical in the district situation. Apart from their traditional authority, medical staff are the highest status members of clinical teams and other key groups. They tended to remain aloof from industrial relations problems, even those they may have caused themselves. It now became even more obvious that medical staff should be more closely concerned in the development of an employee relations policy.

The consultant representative on the DMT was keen to involve his medical colleagues in the affairs of the district, and also to create some understanding of his own dual role of representative and executive on the DMT. Accordingly he, the DPO and the regional training officer designed and mounted a one-day seminar for the chairman of the various medical divisions and senior consultants. The intention of the event was to give the medical staff an appreciation of the current management/staff climate, the direction in which the DMT wished to go, and to draw them closer to the DMT in their thinking and actions on industrial relations.

THE CONSULTANTS' SEMINAR

Twenty-four senior medical staff met the DMT, DPO and the two regional officers in June. Considerable thought had been put into designing the event to have the greatest possible impact. This was most brilliantly accomplished when the DMT consultant representative drew a direct analogy between the clinical model (anatomy–physiology–pathology–investigation–treatment–post mortem) and the industrial relations situation in the district.*

The pattern for the consultants' seminar matched that of the DMT's 'retreat' and the management workshops. An introduction to the objectives of the event was given, followed by a mutual description of the industrial relations scene at national and local level with especial reference to the place and contribution of medical staff. The district administrator introduced the criteria for a healthy district and the DMT led the ensuing discussions. Although some of the consultants saw the situation as totally dependent on factors external to themselves (such as changes in social values or the NHS administrative structure) many recognized the influence that they did have on industrial relations. Amongst the consultants' conclusions from the day were:

a recognition of other interest groups beside medical staff, and the need to take more interest in other disciplines

the need to review the medical representative system to improve communications

the need to simplify, and thereby make more effective the number of organizations representing doctors

the need for the DMT to visit and understand medical staffs' problems at first hand

the possibility of a joint meeting between the medical professional associations and trade union representatives

an agreement to discuss the content and conclusions of the seminar through the medical divisions.

* The author is indebted to Dr. H. Miller for permission to use the clinical model representation of an industrial relations situation.

The dichotomy between the medical group and other disciplines in the district illustrates the need for OD practitioners to be aware of the sets of informal relations in the organization as well as the formal structure. Inter-group relations are critical in the provision of health care, and the consultants' seminar emphasized the need for OD facilitators or trainers to understand and work on inter-group phenomena in the social context of the organization.

Review: April, year three

The DMT had been keeping in touch with the progress of the project through its regular business meetings. However, the DMT decided to fulfil its agreement made during its 'retreat' and hold a review session to consider the whole programme and the inter-relationships of its parts. A whole day was set aside therefore to consider the various changes in the district culture against its objectives of the first year; to consider whether these objectives were still appropriate; and to decide further action if necessary.

A number of factors emerged. In describing the current situation of the district the DMT now had no shared picture of the organization, although most feelings were positive whereas 18 months before they had had common, negative, perceptions. The results of the workshops were agreed to be making many parts of the organization more effective. One important benefit was that the criteria for a healthy district had provided a framework with which to think about, and judge, the current state of employee relations. The employee relations policy was still seen as highly relevant to the Portsmouth health district.

Further areas for action to continue improving the situation were decided. These included the better definition of consultation machinery outside the major hospitals, and increasing the visibility of the DMT. Further intensive negotiating skills training was agreed for negotiating teams in the hospitals (individuals had attended the workshops, not these teams). It was also thought that managers required further appreciation of problem solving and resource utilization techniques. The DMT recognized that most major problems began at its level and agreed first to investigate its own decision-making. The two regional officers have been asked to produce proposals for this diagnosis, including process commentary at DMT meetings.

Postlude

The Portsmouth and South East Hampshire health district project illustrated many principles for the OD oriented trainer. One of the most important of these was that the trainers should not be trapped by the form in which a training request is produced. This project began with a solution, an expectation that

123

training events would be mounted for certain groups of managers. The approach taken by the facilitators and the DMT moved behind the symptoms to more fundamental causes. Training specialists must be able to distinguish between initiatives taken on the training front which attempt to fit people's skills to their roles or aim to remedy organizational problems not soluble by training alone. Whatever the training request, it is likely that there are wider organizational issues which need managing to ensure the complete success of the activity. It should also be noted that the DMT's role was in initiating the employee relations policy, not in imposing it on the management hierarchy. The opportunity was offered to managers in the organization to amend or change this approach. During the workshops policy making became a team experience. This was very different from a normal training approach, which is as a tool of top management in helping those lower in the hierarchy to tackle the problems surrounding them. Similarly, trainers can become either agents for senior management in prescribing for lower managers, or facilitators in improving total organizational effectiveness from the constructive use of management effort at all levels.

In summary, it is possible to describe the Portsmouth project as an OD effort because of the following characteristics:

it is aimed at the total organization
it is management led
the goal is improved organizational effectiveness
it is planned: towards long-term objectives
it is action orientated
it examines not only the tasks and structure of the organization but the attitudes and feelings of employees as well
it is primarily involved with groups
learning activities are mostly experiential and related to the behavioural sciences
it is a continuing, long-term, effort.

In most traditional training programmes the goal is to change others. Trainers, in their own right or as agents of top management, attempt to adapt individual skills and knowledge to fit some prescribed pattern. In this study, the top management group first agreed to change themselves, and then a large mass of senior managers also agreed to change or be party to that change. This produces an irresistible internal pressure towards change in the organization and generates a pressure that is realistically placed to direct and shape its outcomes.

Case study B

THE ROLE OF THE PERSONNEL SPECIALIST IN CHANGING MANAGEMENT DEVELOPMENT IN A MANUFACTURING COMPANY

INTRODUCTION

Personnel managers have the role of expert and also of manager. Large parts of a personnel manager's job have the same problems as any line manager. Notably when introducing a change in personnel systems, he is concerned personally, rather than as an adviser, with the management of change. OD technology can be of material assistance on these occasions.

In some cases, the personnel manager will be responsible for providing specialist technical advice (for example, on the design of a particular grievance procedure, payment system or training programme) but if these are to operate successfully, he must always remember his *responsibility for managing the change involved in their introduction*.

This paper discusses the planning and implementation by the personnel department of a change in a company's management development arrangements for senior managers and directors.

BACKGROUND

The board of a largely autonomous division of approximately 8000* people, comprising 11 heavy manufacturing units, became concerned about the number of external appointments which seemed to be necessary at the most senior levels. In particular, the succession for unit directors and divisional headquarter appointments was unclear. There was a belief that the division should and could be self-sufficient in its management and indeed that some managers could be exported to other divisions.

The division is in a contracting industry but there is substantial challenge and opportunity within rationalized units. Investment continues to be made in modernization programmes.

* Of the 8000 employees in the division, some 2000 are on staff conditions and about 1000 have management responsibility. The directors of each manufacturing unit and their immediate team account for about 110 people.

A manager (the writer) was appointed from outside the company (reporting to the personnel director) to be responsible for management career planning.

THE TECHNICAL APPROACH

After discussion with board members and senior managers, a number of assumptions on which any scheme has to rest became clear. In addition the career development manager and personnel director had strongly held personal convictions about the way that management development should be organized. This had been discussed before I joined the company and clearly it was the wish of the managing director to see these ideas put into practice. It is possible now to list some of these assumptions though at the time they were less categorically expressed:

> managers are responsible for the management of their careers
>
> the directors of the company are responsible for making clear to managers their views on the future of the company and for helping managers to identify possible career opportunities
>
> it is not practical or realistic for the company to indicate specific job or career opportunities at this level of seniority. Individual managers must make their own assessment of possible opportunities.
>
> the management career development function is responsible to both the company and individual managers for creating structures within which the responsibilities of managers and directors can be worked out. The word 'structures' here refers to a set of 'public' expectations created through explicit statements or events made by people holding authority in a relevant area
>
> the company and individual managers have, in the longer term, no allegiance to each other apart from the mutual satisfaction of their needs.

Based on these assumptions the management career development function planned three structures:

1 A series of management assessment courses at which directors would have the opportunity to assess more junior managers and these managers would in turn form judgements about the directors and their views on the company. As a result of this process, it was expected that individual managers would be able to clarify their aspirations in the company

2 The publication of a set of manpower statistics showing age distribution, job tenures at various levels, career paths etc

3 An annual review of the management by the divisional board based on information provided from each of the manufacturing locations and set out in a standardized form.

During the planning process, the necessary staff-work for these three structures was carried out, including the collection and analysis of data for the second item.

PLANNING THE CHANGE PROGRAMME

Having planned for a broad approach to the technical solution of the problem, the personnel director considered how to manage the change in organizational structures and processes which were needed. Using the Clark and Krone[58] map as a base, four areas are seen to need attention relating to structural and process change at individual and company levels.

	Structural	Process
Individual	1	2
Company	4	3

Some of the change goals in each quadrant were:

1 Scheduled training or experience programmes initiated by managers; promotions based on the new management development approach
2 Heightened self-assessment and recognition of areas for possible development for both managers and directors
   recognition of self-motivation dynamics and life goals
3 Improved confidence and trust between directors and potential senior managers as a group
   evolution of corporate future
4 Policy statements on management development structures
   ITB recognition for the 'system'
   credible management development rituals, board reviews etc
   budget provision for management development activities.

It can be seen that the stereotypes of personnel and organization development divide these areas up so that personnel is thought to deal in quadrants 4 and 1 and OD in 2 and 3. In practice, all four quadrants have to be managed if the change to be introduced is to have continuing significance and to achieve permanence. In each area, change will occur if there is some vision of a different way of doing things *and* some dissatisfaction with the present situation *and* there are some practical first steps visible. All three of these criteria need to be met. If any of them is absent, change cannot occur. Finally, it was necessary to consider what power to influence people existed in the personnel department. It is clear that it is necessary for individuals in the organization to be able to have some vision of a future situation, to be dissatisfied with the present one and to see the practical steps. In reality, the difficulty is to achieve sufficient organizational priority for these matters to be considered with some care. For us in the personnel department power to influence people to listen to our ideas depends on how much the person you wish to influence wants something you have. A checklist of things we might have available to influence managers was:

knowledge
resources
group pressures or values
authority or law
charisma or dependence.

Our capacity to influence different managers varied. For instance, for some, the authority of a divisional officer would suffice. Others who would be affected by the proposition thought that they ought to do something 'to conform to best practice'. Some others would have clearly been delighted to change provided the necessary resources could be made available. In practice, lack of authority and/or resources are great obstacles (though having them is no guarantee of success) and so it is wise to pursue these as a first step.

IMPLEMENTATION

Having completed analyses of

the technical problem
the changes in structure and process that were desirable
the authority and power we had to bring about these changes

the process planning was complete.

It is at this stage that the personnel manager and the OD consultant typically part company. The OD consultant is concerned to advise his client and to support him during the action phase. The personnel manager, having planned the needed system in his role as 'expert', must now go on and carry out the line role and manage the change himself. He changes role from expert to manager.[59] In my experience it was at this stage that things began to get rather untidy and opportunistic. Despite a clear view of what was required, I did not find it possible to progress in an orderly and scheduled way for most of the time. In fact, I shared much of the inability of line managers to describe exactly what I did at any particular time! After some time, sufficient people had shared a vision of 'what might be', and were sufficiently dissatisfied with the present situation, that a practical first proposal could be agreed and the change process could begin brick by brick.

Through the establishment of a management assessment course, quadrants 2 then 3 were changed. After some experience of these courses a policy was written and published and some external recognition for the system was achieved through the ITB, Finally, it became possible to produce individual training programmes and to effect the formal succession and promotion systems in the business.

At present, there is activity in all four quadrants simultaneously and a new equilibrium has been achieved. Not all that we hoped for has been achieved and further changes will be necessary to improve and refine the fundamental change. It is very easy during this phase to lose sight of the overall direction and become too much concerned with individual people and cases. I tried to ensure that I reviewed where I had moved to with a disinterested party in order to make this clear to myself. Perhaps it is in this role that a second level consultant is best used.

We have now reached a point where most of the initial objectives have been achieved. I failed to create a vision or dissatisfaction with respect to the manpower planning aspects of the scheme because the information I had to offer was already rather widely known. It proved impossible to influence people to put up cash for information which they considered already available albeit in a less easily accessible form. Hence the present arrangements continue but otherwise many of our original hopes have been put into practice.

CONCLUSIONS

The personnel manager, like many others today, is required to fill a double role. He must be a professional technical expert, able to advise others on the legal implications of decisions and on the most efficient solutions to particular problems. In addition, he has a management role and will face all the problems of introducing changes to the business. Skill in using change technology can help him in his own job and enhance his authority to advise other managers concerning what might be the most appropriate change strategies for them.

Case study C

ESTABLISHING A PERMANENT OD ROLE IN THE PERSONNEL FUNCTION OF BAT (UK AND EXPORT) LTD

THE COMPANY

BAT (UK and Export) is a recently formed and wholly owned subsidiary company of BAT Industries Ltd, which is itself a newly formed (holding) company for the diverse interests of the former BAT Company Ltd. The parent company is one of the largest in the UK and, by virtue of its turnover, is listed in *The Times* top 1000 British enterprises. It has a history of rapid expansion since its formation in 1902. Part of this expansion has been in the 'export' from the UK of tobacco products and the last 10 years have seen significant changes in this part of the parent company's operations. This culminated in 1976 with the move to legal company status. The numerous changes that were made over the years called for extensive alterations in the internal organization of what is now the UK and Export Company. The creation of new locations, new functions (including personnel), and the demand for new roles and skills meant the organization had to adapt to a variety of changes over a relatively short time.

Although the BAT Group has a history of working with OD skills BAT (UK and Export) has been developing a distinctive approach to suit its own particular circumstances. This is a brief description of the formulation of that approach.

OD IN THE BAT GROUP

In order to understand fully the OD role in BAT (UK and Export) it is necessary to have some knowledge of the way OD was introduced and grew in the BAT Group. The size and complexity of the group has always required that particular attention be paid to fostering the management skills vital to the successful operation of such an organization. The number of managers, for example, some 700 'British' International staff, has always meant a sizeable resourcing problem in terms of logistics alone. Nevertheless, much of the effort towards management development has been undertaken at the individual level based on succession planning. This ensured that each individual received a pattern of different (geographical, functional and so on), experiences at different and appropriate stages of his or her career.

The scale of the company's management training needs led in the early 1950s to the setting up of a company management training centre at Chelwood in Essex. As well as providing Conference facilities this Management Centre provides internal staff training resources commensurate with the company's needs. A good example of the type of programme undertaken at Chelwood is the four-week senior management development programme which combines lectures, by both external and senior company speakers, with experiential exercises aimed at improving performance in the job.

Although management training and development was seen as part of the personnel function in the group, the special status and complexity of management development, in some instances, led to a separation of the development experience from the company's needs as perceived by the personnel administrators and others. The rise of OD in the group reflected this perception.

In the period 1958 to 1965 the various theories of Drucker, McGregor and Herzberg had been believed to describe the basis of a 'total management philosophy' which was appropriate to the BAT Group. However, in the event, this did not lead to a sufficient depth of understanding and degree of application that was satisfactory so far as the company was concerned. This realization coincided with the introduction and growth of Blake's managerial grid[60] as a basis for developing managers within the organization. In the early 1960s small samples of managers in various divisions had experimented with the grid. As a belief in this approach developed and especially after Blake and Mouton had themselves run a seminar for a group of very senior managers and main board directors in July 1965 it was decided that a comprehensive training programme based on the grid should be undertaken.

Up to the time of writing and since the first seminar was run in 1965 approximately 1500 managers have taken part in one-week grid seminars. The courses were most frequently run at the Chelwood establishment with line managers acting as tutors backed up by Chelwood instructors and occasionally outside consultants. The grid seminars were often undertaken as a preliminary to the four-week management development programme. By the early 1970s some doubts were being expressed about the overall effectiveness of the grid seminars in terms of the company's needs at the time. It was believed by some that too few managers were translating the grid concepts into action and that the courses by themselves were not permeating sufficiently to stimulate fundamental corporate development. There was no doubt that the interest and commitment concerning the grid was not anywhere near as high as it had been. A growing number of people saw management by objectives (MBO)[61] as being more appropriate. This was especially so in the case of the international exports division (IED) which was later to become BAT (UK and Export).

In the early 1960s IED was one of the 'guinea pigs' for the Blake programme. Following its introduction, every manager in IED underwent the introductory phase one seminar and considerable progress was made with the phase two working team development seminars as well as other phases. The success in restructuring the department to a division (which took place before the further move to legal company status) and the new business directions that were developed at this time were attributed largely to the effective use of the Blake models. But whereas the programme had resulted in a far greater degree of 'candour and openness' about the purpose of the department in London, the response of the factories in Liverpool and Southampton had been different. The factories' interest was focused on attitudes concerning management authority. It was believed that there were alternative ways of managing and that quite definitely the human relationships existing between manager and subordinate significantly affected the results achieved. The management of the factories therefore believed this was the area where further study and development work should be concentrated.

Eventually, in 1970, a 'marriage' between the factories and the London section of IED took place. One outcome of this was the large commitment made to a two-year MBO programme run by outside consultants. The emphasis in this programme was much more on results at the individual manager level. Increasingly attempts were to be made to define links between organizational objectives and different managers together with a formalization of the resulting plans and an analysis relevant to the division and its operating circumstances.

The next significant step in the history of the OD role came in 1975 when the personnel director of the newly formed BAT (UK and Export) company commissioned a study of how the organization was currently managing its development and of how the personnel resource could best contribute. A survey was designed primarily to examine the current operation of the manpower development sequence as practised by the 35 most senior managers in the company. This included top management in both factories. Data were obtained primarily through interviews with each manager. These were semi-structured around various key decisions in the manpower development sequence. The interviewer was introduced by the personnel director to each manager concerned and dates were arranged to suit their convenience. The interviews took place in the managers' own offices and the interviewer took notes which were later summarized as the basis for the final report to the personnel director. The most important conclusions of this report highlighted a number of important organization problems:

1 relationships between BAT (UK and Export) and the Tobacco Division of the group were still in a state of some confusion, especially at senior level

2 there remained some unresolved issues concerning the new and future role for BAT (UK and Export) at board level
3 in the absence of totally clear direction, each function tended to 'do its own thing' with inadequate attention being paid to the needs of other functions
4 although it was accepted that this confusion would exist for a period, the pressures of the change, and the ability of current management staff to respond were tending towards deterioration rather than development.

As well as drawing attention to these significant organization problems, the report pointed out some important features of the potential for development. For example, as most of the managers were 'career staff' a high degree of informal organization existed. In some circumstances this had enabled adaptation to take place more readily when crises had occurred.

In the light of this report the personnel director was able to identify and define the need for organization development skills. Furthermore, the need was identified and defined in terms of a permanent position within the organization and located in the personnel function. It was believed that this was the best site for a resource which would work continually on fundamental organizational problems. This decision was undoubtedly facilitated by the previous developmental activities undertaken in BAT and by the progress made by the personnel function which had established itself as a firm professional presence in industrial relations, personnel administration, the organization of training and the development of the company's human resources.

The purpose of the OD role was defined as 'improving the contribution of organization to business success in BAT (UK and Export)'. It was to be concerned primarily with the total company organization as well as working at departmental or functional level. It was to look at both internal affairs and external relationships. Interventions would be primarily at board level. The role would also be concerned (where this did not cut across the main aim) with the rest of the senior management of the company. Another vital aspect of the early OD role that was established concerned the skills that were considered of paramount importance. It was believed that the OD resource would have to be business rather than solely behavioural science oriented and that it would have to be capable of adapting to the particular style of the organization rather than vice-versa. 'Process' involvement in on-going problems was thought to be more likely to succeed than heavily structured learning exercises. This certainly proved to be so and much of the early work of the OD role took place through process consultation in the on-going flow of management work. This approach resulted in problems being tackled which were often significantly different from those diagnosed in the survey. The OD manager believed that it could be more productive to operate in this way. Furthermore, in the early stages interventions tended to address perceived problems that the senior managers were willing to seek help with. Thus, *initially*, the 'planned change programme' consisted largely of opportunistic responses to 'felt needs' on the part of individual senior managers.

The kinds of activity which took place in the early stages ranged from participating in departmental annual conferences, helping on major reorganizations in particular functions, working on individual managers' problems and specific group and teamwork activities. The OD role was also concerned in the implementation and development of the current formal personnel systems and was involved most directly with the planning and development of human resources, for example, succession planning, job definition and performance appraisal.

Thus the main purpose of these initial stages of the OD programme may be briefly summarized as to work in each function so as to establish the credibility of the OD role. The aim was to generate sufficient confidence amongst the senior managers about OD so that they would be willing to see it used to address more general and more fundamental problems. This strategy worked and it eventually became possible to establish a more comprehensive and direct change programme.

PLANNED CHANGE

One of the most important priorities of the managing director at BAT (UK and Export) was the establishment of more rational and systematic methods for understanding and taking decisions about the company's business. The managing director's own strategy for achieving this was to direct a lot of time and energy towards 'planning' throughout the organization. It proved possible to establish an OD role in this development of planning. This may be attributed to the growing credibility of OD and to the work of the personnel function in general in creating greater understanding of how more effective human resource planning could help resolve major organizational problems.

Some managers had at this time suggested that setting up a separate planning function would be the best way to resolve the planning issue. The OD role made a key intervention at this point by questioning this suggestion. It was pointed out that this would be an abdication of a key management task and that there were many advantages to be gained from ensuring a continued line management concern in planning. In any case, the knowledge possessed by individual managers about their own operations usually made them the best people to take a lead in planning. The OD role argued that a separate planning function could compound the communication and co-operation problems rather than help overcome them.

The short-term solution eventually adopted throughout the organization was the creation of cross-departmental and functional teams of line managers. It was to be the job of these teams to analyse and develop planning and co-ordination. Whereas the management services function took the responsibility for providing the formal framework for the range and nature of decisions involved in the total planning operation, the OD role now had the opportunity of intervening in the process of this decision making through its work with the various teams. This was highly important in terms of the contribution that OD could make to the improvement of the organization's day-to-day operations. Although the planning may have been concerned with the future, many of the issues that had to be resolved by the planning teams in deciding on future actions inevitably led to them addressing existing problems of co-operation and effective decision making.

The work on the planning exercises led directly to another key OD intervention. Throughout the evolution of the organization the Board of Management had been concerned to identify opportunities for developing its own operation. Whereas the individual roles of the members of the board had been primarily as functional heads, it had become increasingly clear that in order to provide effective and unified direction for the company *as a whole* some team work development needed to be undertaken. This was achieved through process interventions by the OD resource into the ongoing business of the team. It started with interventions in the planning deliberations and built up eventually into a full-blown team development programme involving not only process consultancy but off-site workshops and several other activities. Through the development of a more effective process for managing the business at this level it then became possible to identify and develop programmes for other key management levels and areas.

CONCLUSIONS

An attempt has been made here to outline one particular company's experience of creating a working relationship between organization development skills and the more traditional tools used by the personnel function in carrying out its duties. Although this relationship will continue to evolve, a sufficient measure of progress has been achieved for some conclusions to be drawn.

Some part of the progress achieved may be attributed to the individuals concerned but the present writer would maintain that other 'institutional' factors have been highly important. Perhaps the most important of these was the multi-national context, where the very size of the enterprise makes organization, as a skill, of great importance. In these circumstances extra effort had to be made to help individual members of the organization understand and fulfil their role in the enterprise. Another important institutional factor in this case was the particular circumstances of BAT (UK and Export) where change in business operations had led to needs for organizational change, either building new organization resources or developing old ones. Perhaps the most important factor of all was long standing recognition within BAT as a whole of the need for a specialized and professional personnel function. In BAT (UK and Export) particularly this led to the establishment of an important (director level representation) and well regarded personnel department within the company. This provided a sound basis for gaining acceptance of the contribution that OD skills might make to the company's effectiveness.

Finally, it is possible to draw some general conclusions about the operation of OD in organization. On the evidence of this case study it is this writer's opinion that the body of knowledge and methodology that OD practitioners are currently seeking to establish can undoubtedly allow the personnel function to play a fuller and more influential role in the organization. For example, if the personnel function contains people with skills and knowledge relevant to organization then it will be, and it will be seen to be, well equipped to help the organization make better decisions, improve communication, set more suitable goals and generally increase its effectiveness. However, for this to happen it will mean that the personnel function must master the general principles, if not the local details, associated with other functions and particularly those of other key decision makers in the enterprise. In this way the OD role can, to some extent, have features in common with the other professional and service functions where specialized methods have been built up to handle particular problems.

This conception of the potential contribution of the OD role may be a little ahead of the professionalization of OD itself. A vital ingredient of the success of the work done in BAT (UK and Export) was the way in which OD was practised, that is by using the perceptions, ideas and language of the organization and its managers rather than rigidly holding to theory or demanding the ideal. It would have been of little use to employ language and ideas which were only comprehensible to the OD practitioner. In this case study, despite the acknowledged excellence of Blake's models and the participation by all the managers concerned in the resulting programmes, the concepts were rarely used by these managers for understanding and tackling existing organizational problems. A good manager usually has his own theories. The problem of generating learning between his own individual theories and the ideals of such as Blake must not be underestimated.

Case study D

TEAM INTRODUCTION WORKSHOPS: A METHOD OF SPEEDING UP THE INTEGRATION OF NEW TEAM MEMBERS

THE ORGANIZATIONAL BACKGROUND

The events described here were part of a company-wide organization development activity in a large operating unit (5000 employees) of a multi-national group in the petro-chemical industry. The writer and a colleague formed a two-man team of OD advisors situated in the personnel function of the organization. The management staff of the organization were drawn from a wide range of national backgrounds including Asian, English, Australian, Swiss, Dutch, German and French. This fact suggests that the activities described here are suitable for use across several cultures.

At the time these workshops began to be carried out, the organization development activity had already been underway for two years. This is important as, by this time, about 30 per cent of the senior staff had been exposed to a five day residential training programme aimed at developing greater interpersonal skills and self-awareness. In fact, several of the managers who subsequently attended or requested team introduction workshops had not experienced the five day programme, but the culture in the organization was sufficiently attuned to the value of building speedy and strong working relationships that they became a regular part of the organization's activities.

There is little disagreement these days amongst managers and personnel specialists about the critical importance of the smooth functioning team for the continued survival and growth of an organization. This is even more true if that organization has a complex and sophisticated technology and political structure, as in the case being discussed here. In spite of this general agreement it is rather ironic that those very sophisticated management and career development systems devised by personnel departments to resource the organization have themselves created serious problems for the maintenance of stable work teams. Managers are moved around on planned assignments for broadening and promotion, often not staying more than two to four years (as happened in the company described here). This clearly has benefits for the organization and the individual but it can also be extremely disruptive for work teams who are

137

constantly having to re-adjust to new members and new bosses. It was this need to re-adjust quickly and effectively that led to the development of team introduction workshops in the client company.

THE ISSUES INVOLVED IN JOINING A NEW TEAM

In the company being discussed here there was a management team of eight members. The likelihood of that team remaining intact for more than nine months to one year was remote. In some cases of similar teams in the company there were three or four changes of membership in one year. This meant that at frequent intervals in the team's life energy was diverted away from task accomplishment and directed at coping with the problems of new membership. In this case the new arrival was a fresh managing director. This fact made the problems of integration potentially more acute.

It is useful to look at this kind of situation from two perspectives; from the point of view of the new member and from that of the awaiting team. For any new managing director the greatest pressure is the need to form new relationships at high speed so that he can concentrate on his key organizational tasks with the best possible co-operation from his new team members. Even if his new role and task is similar to previous ones, as it was in this case, the environment in which it is to be carried out is different and the need to form good working relationships quickly is critical. In the receiving community, too, there is a degree of coping behaviour visible well before the actual arrival of the new boss. In this particular case, for example, important policy and operational decisions were being avoided or delayed until it became clearer which way the wind would blow. Also, considerable energy was being channelled into investigating and discussing the previous known history and track record of the new arrival, especially his preferences for ways of doing things, management style, likes and dislikes and so on. Consequently, task performance in the organization visibly suffers and a mythological picture exists in the system before the man arrives. This more often than not bears little relation to reality but it nevertheless forms a basis for behaviour patterns towards him when he arrives.

For the new arrival himself similar anxieties and concerns exist and much of his energy in the early stages of the new assignment can also be diverted into coping with issues at two distinct levels, the intellectual and task level and, secondly, the personal relationship or emotional level (often described in the jargon as 'task' level and 'process' level). The former concerns give rise to such questions as:

How competent are the team members?

How much skill and knowledge can they bring to the problems we will face?
How able are these people at decision making and problem solving?

The emotional level questions focus around such questions as:

What sort of role, behaviour, style should I adopt in this team?
How do I want to be seen?
Will my needs, values, beliefs coincide or clash with those of the team members?
How much power will I have and how should I exercise it?

These issues and anxieties exist, whether or not they are recognized consciously. Under normal circumstances they are coped with quite satisfactorily over a period (often as long as six to 12 months after the arrival of a new boss). Any acceleration in this coping/assimilation process will minimize the more disruptive effects of such changes on the working of the organization. One way of doing this is to create a vehicle for the sharing of some of the issues, concerns and expectations, both at the task and personal level as early as possible in the new relationship so that myth and fantasy can be tested against reality without the work of the organization being adversely affected in the process. It was to this end that the team introduction workshop was developed.

TEAM INTRODUCTION WORKSHOPS

Each group situation, task and new member is different. Workshops need to be custom built to reflect these differences but the fundamental approach and overall objectives will be the same.

The object is to help develop a closer understanding between the newcomer and the group he is joining by sharing, in a structural way, perceptions, expectations, values and ideas about themselves, each other and the tasks they will be tackling together. In this way relationships in the team will be based right from the start on available facts rather than hearsay, stereotypes and mythology. The workshop achieved this by focusing on three specific areas:

1 the group displays to the newcomer how they see the group currently operating as a team eg values, norms, strengths, weaknesses
2 the group and the newcomer share expectations about each other
3 the group and the newcomer discuss current task priorities for the group.

The time required for such workshops varies from one to two days depending on the needs of the group, the wishes of the newcomer, and the time each is prepared to devote to the activity. With less than two full days (16 hours) available it is my experience that the objectives have to be curtailed either to concentrate on the personal relationships aspects or the task priorities aspect. Either seems to work reasonably well but dealing with them separately is not as effective as spending time on both. In the example cited here an attempt was made to cover both aspects in one day (10 hours), but in the event little time was devoted to task related aspects and they formed the basis of further meetings at a later date.

INTRODUCING A NEW MANAGING DIRECTOR—A PROTOTYPE WORKSHOP

The overall objective of the one day workshop was to integrate a new managing director with his management team of seven functional managers (heads of operations, finance, personnel, technical director etc.). It took place in the managing director's office. The location of the workshop was felt to be important. It was known that it would be valuable if the workshop was seen as 'work' activity rather than 'training' or 'personnel' activity, and the normal meeting place of the team was the obvious choice to reinforce this point. Another reason for choosing the managing director's office was that the role and structure of the group could be demonstrated in the same way as it would be at normal work meetings in the future. This issue is sometimes avoided in off-site sessions in my experience due to a tendency for members to deny status differences and 'pretend' that a kind of pseudo-equality exists. This is unreal and therefore commitments entered into look rather different back in the 'cold light' of the boss's office. They therefore subsequently fade away.

The specific objectives of the workshop were set out as follows:

1 To increase the 'visibility' of the managing director to the team
   (a) as a person
   (b) as a manager
2 To increase the 'visibility' of the team to the managing director
   (a) as individuals
   (b) as subordinate managers
   (c) as a working group
3 To explore problems existing
   (a) within the team itself
   (b) within the total organization.

It was also hoped that at the end of the day a level of commitment would be achieved towards tackling some of the issues which had surfaced during the workshop.

The session began with a 10-minute introductory talk by the consultants. (Two consultants worked with this group since it was a prototype workshop but under other circumstances one is quite adequate.) This consisted of a brief review of the concepts of group development and the differences between task and process (most of the group were reasonably familiar with these ideas) a statement of objectives and a suggested timetable for the day. This was followed by a brief period of questioning and clarification, after which all members of the team present were asked to draw on a piece of paper a line representing their own expected length of life from birth to death and then to mark with an X the point where they were now, thus splitting the line into life-past and life-future. On this line they were asked to put a letter L at that point which represented the lowest ebb of their life and a letter H to represent the highest point of their life. Under the line they were asked to write a per cent figure representing their current level of morale.

In answer to a number of questions at this point it was explained that high and low points could be events already experienced in the past or expected in the future (for one or two the L point was some years hence at the point of retirement). It was also pointed out that they could relate to career, family, hobbies or a combination of all three depending on the person's own situation. On completing this the members of the group were asked to share their data in turn, giving any explanation or elaboration they felt necessary. During this part of the exercise a firm rule was laid down that, although a member could ask any question he liked of another, however personal, the respondent had the right to refuse to answer and close-off that avenue of enquiry. This was done to minimize the risk of individuals feeling pushed into a corner and becoming defensive. One of the norms that needed to be established early on was that it was 'OK to say "No".'

This exercise was aimed at 'unfreezing' the group and acting as a vehicle for some personal information sharing beyond the normally 'accepted' level amongst managers in the organization. In fact it generated a surprising amount of very personal data which increased the 'visibility' of the team and the managing director to each other. An additional bonus was that the existing team members were finding out much more about each other's fears and ambitions than they had ever known before. Having increased members' personal visibility, and taken a step towards establishing a level of trust in the group through information sharing, the second task was begun.

Each member of the group was provided with a large piece of newsprint and a felt-tipped pen. Pre-printed across the top of the managing director's sheet were the words, 'As a manager I demand subordinates who . . .'. Whilst the rest of the group received sheets stating: 'As a subordinate I want a manager who . . .'. All participants were asked to complete the sentence using five different words or phrases which would indicate their preferred way of managing or being managed. As the sentences were completed the sheets were posted around the walls of the office and members circulated and read the lists. If anyone came across a statement on a list that he wished to discuss, clarify or take issue with he was asked to initial the statement. The lists were then discussed with special reference to those statements with the most initials. Not surprisingly the managing director's list was the most heavily subscribed and a useful opportunity was created to explore some of his values, philosophies and beliefs about managing.

The focus of the workshop now moved from the individual to the work group, and the members of the group (excluding the managing director) were asked to list five adjectives which, for them personally, described the team and its salient characteristics. They were also asked to put a mark by any items on their list which they regarded as negative influences. This data was again posted on the walls together with the results of a brief team development scale questionnaire which had been administered and analysed before the workshop (see Appendix 2). A discussion followed during which priorities were agreed concerning areas in which the members of the team wanted to improve their way of working together and a commitment was made to take action upon these in the near future.

Finally, each member of the group was asked to write down (again excluding the managing director) the three major tasks, problems or opportunities currently facing the organization and on which, as a policy making team, they needed to work. The results were posted, in groups according to similarity, ranked according to priority and commitments made to work through them as agenda items at future policy meetings.

At this point the workshop ended and during the following week all the data were collated and analysed by the consultants and fed back in the form of an *aide memoire* to each member of the group. This included some suggestions for future action over and above those clearly emerging from the workshop. (An edited version of the data emerging from the workshop and the consultants' comments appears at the end of this paper in the shape of the *aide memoire*).

EVALUATION OF THE WORKSHOP

In evaluating the experience seven of the eight members thought that the experience had been helpful and constructive in its results and that it would have a positive impact on the future working of the team. Asked to indicate their feelings on a five-point scale covering four areas, the results were:

1 Overall value of workshop (0–5)   3.5
2 Amount of progress made during day (0–5)   3.0
3 Degree of participation (0–5)   4.0
4 Level of trust and frankness in discussion (0–5)   3.0

Two other significant events also followed some months later as a direct result of the workshop. The managing director allocated three days during the normal working week for further team development and the team took part in a development workshop at an off-site place. This was aimed at increasing their awareness and social skills in interpersonal and small group relationships; also, the team introduction workshop was repeated later on for the arrival of a new replacement member of the team.

SUMMARY

Several such workshops have now been requested and run since the one described here. They have all been found useful by the groups concerned, especially as a way to begin the integration process with only a relatively small amount of time available. Clearly, there will be increasing applicability for this sort of activity in organizations as the need for greater flexibility and more temporary teams grows. As Bennis claims:

> There will . . . be reduced commitment to work groups . . . while skills in human interaction will become more important due to the growing need for collaboration in complex tasks . . . People will have to learn to develop quick and intense relationships on the job and learn to bear the loss of more enduring work relationships. Coping with rapid change, living in the temporary work systems, setting up (in quick-step time) meaningful relations—and then breaking those all auger social strains and psychological tensions.[62]

The work described here was intended to go a small way towards minimizing the duration and effect of some of these strains in one company. I am convinced it can be replicated elsewhere to good effect, provided it is handled in a common-sense, thoughtful way.

AIDE MEMOIRE SUMMARIZING WORKSHOP DATA

At the end of the session we agreed to write-up the data from the meeting and feed it back to you as an *aide memoire*. You will find attached three Appendices each with the recorded responses from the various exercises.

Appendix 1 Demands and requests
          As a manager I would like . . . As a subordinate I want . . .
     2 Self-perception of management team
     3 Major problems/tasks facing the company

In addition we have attached some notes which attempt to crystallize our thoughts arising out of that meeting and which we feel point towards some future action areas for the management group.

TWO FUNDAMENTAL ISSUES

For some time now the management group has been gradually moving quite consciously towards a team model of managing the business. Our observations of the group at work at the team introduction workshop, our previous knowledge of the group at work and the data generated at the meeting, consistently lead us to the belief that the group is currently vacillating between two distinct models of managing. These models are shown diagramatically below:

A *Functional model*   B *Team (linking pin) model*

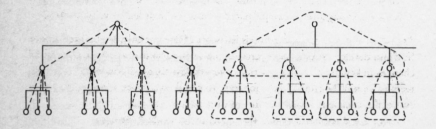

In model A, the manager has one clear role. He forms a link in a vertical communication and authority chain. He manages his function and is accountable to the chief executive for that.

In model B, the manager has two distinct roles:

Role 1 as a functional manager, exactly as in Model A
     2 as a co-member of the managing group where he becomes jointly accountable for team actions and decisions, and is the link between that team and his own function.

The task and behavioural characteristics of these two roles are different and need constantly to be unscrambled.

There are very real difficulties inherent in attempting to shift from a style of operating which is relatively clear and simple, towards one that is more ambiguous, more demanding personally and professionally, and more time consuming. From the data generated in the session and the follow-up comments, it seems to us that you as a group and as individuals are experiencing some of those difficulties. This shows up in the wide diversity of values and beliefs expressed, the wide range of perceptions about the team and the uncertainty expressed in the team perception adjectives (see Appendix 3).

We think that two fundamental issues around this area need to be worked through and decisions taken in the group. These issues are:

1 Do we *need*, for the effective management of the company's operations, to operate the 'B' model?
2 Do I *want*, as an individual, to work in a 'B' model?

Following from these questions are a range of questions and implications of which the critical ones seem to be:

1 If it is chosen to concentrate on developing a 'B' model of managing, what are the positive steps needed to do that, and how much time is necessary/are we willing, to give to that development?
2 What are the implications for individual behaviour, skills and risk taking if we go that way and are we prepared to accept, or at least live with those?

At present the management group is in a state of flux not only due to its efforts to find and develop an effective operating mode but also due to a large number of changes in key membership positions over the last six to nine months. For these reasons we feel the time is right for steps to be taken to work through the issues and make decisions about the future direction of the team.

There are three basic phases that need to be worked through:

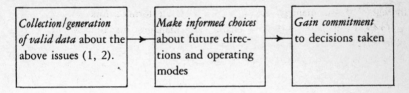

| Collection/generation of *valid data* about the above issues (1, 2). | → | Make informed choices about future directions and operating modes | → | Gain commitment to decisions taken |

We look forward to the opportunity of discussing these observations and ideas with you whenever you wish, either as individuals or as a group.

APPENDIX 1

DEMANDS AND REQUESTS

'As a manager I would like subordinates who'.

    communicate freely with me and with each other
    are technically competent
    are interested in the poeple who are working for them

have a span of interest beyond their own jobs
have a sense of humour

'As a subordinate I want a manager who':

I respect as a person professionally and 'individually'
lets me get on with my job on the basis of mutually agreed terms of reference
is interested, has input, and challenges me and therefore encourages
    mutuality
will share his experience and help me grow
wants results and will tell me when I fail, and why, and when I succeed
is open
states his objectives clearly
motivates me by working on my strong points
is prepared to accept his own responsibilities
is prepared to trust his organization
establishes policies and objectives with me
expects reporting on an exception basis only
honest and open
competent
backs up own staff
explains clearly and concisely his requirements of the various parts of his
    organization
can offer criticism unemotionally and with clear intention
sets yardsticks for guidance on extent of reporting back expected
communicates downwards
motivates
defines clearly my objectives
gives clear terms of reference
is able to give guidance where necessary
can balance, judge more and less important subjects
can stimulate
has time to listen to my problems
can explain 'why' he wants things done
does not try to 'shave budgets'
can laugh at himself (sometimes)
delegates clearly defined bracket of responsibilities to me
is willing to consider suggestions and recommendations
is interested in people—in me and my co-workers
backs me up after having said 'yes' to a certain course of action
has a clear line—policies are well defined

As far as it is possible to categorize the above statements, three areas of major concern are very apparent:

clarity of objectives and responsibilities (nine mentions)
challenge (five mentions)
trust, openness (four mentions)

These are areas which most of the team see as key factors for them in a boss.

APPENDIX 2

SELF-PERCEPTIONS OF MANAGEMENT TEAM

The team development scale as filled in before the meeting has been reproduced here, together with the adjectives used by members to describe the team.

Team development scale

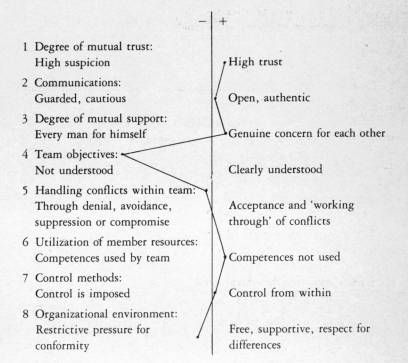

− +

1 Degree of mutual trust:
High suspicion — High trust

2 Communications:
Guarded, cautious — Open, authentic

3 Degree of mutual support:
Every man for himself — Genuine concern for each other

4 Team objectives:
Not understood — Clearly understood

5 Handling conflicts within team:
Through denial, avoidance, suppression or compromise — Acceptance and 'working through' of conflicts

6 Utilization of member resources:
Competences used by team — Competences not used

7 Control methods:
Control is imposed — Control from within

8 Organizational environment:
Restrictive pressure for conformity — Free, supportive, respect for differences

Perceptions of management team

OPEN	THAWING	LIMITED
CONSTRUCTIVE	AWAKENING	SOCIALLY FRIENDLY
WILLING	CAUTIOUS	CONSERVATIVE
SUCCESSFUL	UNCERTAIN	AMATEUR
(MODERATELY)	WAITING	HUMOURLESS
BASICALLY	HESITANT	TIME CONSUMING
CONSTRUCTIVE	MODERATELY	CONSTRICTED
	CONFUSED	
	MIXED-UP	
	UNSTRUCTURED	
	HAPHAZARD	

←——————————————————————————————————→

'Positive'   'Neutral'   'Negative'

We have grouped the adjectives used roughly into apparent positive and negative columns, and in fact we found that the majority fell firmly in the middle group.

APPENDIX 3

MAJOR PROBLEMS/TASKS FACING COMPANY (AS IDENTIFIED BY MANAGEMENT TEAM IN WORKSHOP)

Each of the managers had been asked to list, in order of priority, the three most important issues and tasks which the management team ought to tackle. The following are some of the issues and tasks that were listed (some have been removed as they were specific or confidential to the company concerned). A summary of the rankings is also given.

Manpower forecasting guidelines
Policies/objectives vis à vis government
Objectives (establish tasks/targets for next four years)
Assessment of resources required for next four years
Adjust planning to circumstances
Develop trust in management team
Regionalization
Improve efficiency of management team
Improve communication up and down the line

Summary ranking:

Ranking	No of mentions
(1) Manpower forecasting	4
(2) Corporate objectives/team targets	3
(3) Develop management team	2
(4) Relations/policies vis à vis government	2

Biographical notes on contributors

Marjo van Boeschoten Director of Social Ecology Associates Ltd, a member-company of Nederland Pedagogische Institut (NPI) International. Before he came to the UK, he worked with NPI in Holland and co-ordinated the Amsterdam docks OD project. He worked as a personnel director in Dutch industry for 12 years before undertaking his work in NPI.

John Bristow Currently self-employed as a consultant, researcher and trainer for organization and management development, specializing in the area of industrial relations. He worked for two years on a project in the development of industrial relations at local level within BOC (Gases) Ltd. Previously he worked for five years at the National Institute for Industrial Psychology.

Keith Carby After working as a researcher at the University of London, he joined the IPM as Executive Officer, Training, Organization and Manpower Planning, where he was responsible for the Institute's activities over a wide range of subjects including OD. He is currently on the research staff of Ashridge Management College, working within companies on the management of change. Keith Carby is a co-opted member of the Institute's National Committee for Organization and Manpower Planning and an adviser to the IPM's major job redesign project.

Arthur Chapman At present Executive Director—Personnel, Trebor Sharps Ltd, Arthur Chapman has worked in training in Pilkingtons and the (former) British Motor Corporation. He has also held the post of Personnel Development Manager with Esso Petroleum Company Ltd.

Malcolm Leary Staff member of Social Ecology Associates involved in development, counselling, and research in organizational and social life. Formerly, he worked in the steel industry and then for the Food, Drink and Tobacco Industry Training Board as Senior Training Adviser, where he had special responsibility for the development of industrial relations.

Eric Mitchell Formerly with ICI Ltd where he was involved in implementing the weekly staff agreement and the staff development programme. Later as a

150

member of Philip's central technical, efficiency and organization department, he worked on job evaluation, harmonization of conditions of employment and work structuring. Eric Mitchell was until recently on contract to the Work Research Unit where he was a senior consultant. He is presently Organization and Manpower Development Manager with BAT (UK and Export) Ltd.

Mike Pedler Senior Lecturer, Regional Management Centre, Sheffield Polytechnic. He previously worked with Procter and Gamble and the British Steel Corporation. He has worked as a consultant with a number of British and international organizations on industrial relations and management development.

Roger Plant After working in personnel and industrial relations in the motor and light engineering industries, Roger Plant joined Shell as Organization Development Consultant, first in the UK and later in the Far East. He has been consultant to companies in Singapore, Australia, USA as well as the UK and is now Assistant Director of Studies at Ashridge Management College.

Jeremy Ridge After a research project in ICI Ltd on organization and communication problems, he worked on a number of OD projects in the company, leading to a post in the OD unit at head office. He then joined BAT (UK and Export) where he was concerned with institutionalizing OD concepts and technology within the personnel function. He is now working with PA Management Consultants.

Rod Scarth At present Training Manager, RHM Cereals Ltd. His previous experience has included responsibilities for management and organization development at the Food, Drink and Tobacco Industry Training Board and Shell Research Ltd. He also worked at the National Institute of Industrial Psychology for three years on selection testing and counselling.

Graham Smith For the last two years with the Wessex Regional Health Authority as Regional Training and Education Officer. His special interests, about which he has published several articles, are the empowerment of employees to take initiatives in large organizations; the practicability and cultural transferability of OD methodologies and techniques; and the relationships between organizations and their environments.

Manab Thakur After working in personnel and training in England and in India he gained research and teaching experience, mainly in the area of organizational behaviour. He is the author of several publications in the UK on various aspects of personnel management. Manab Thakur worked for the IPM for four years as Research Officer until his recent move to the United States, where he is now teaching and researching at the Eastern Kentucky University. One of his current research projects is a cross-cultural study of British and American experience of managerial rewards.

Brian Wilson His previous work with ICI Ltd was concerned with the behavioural and systems aspects of organizational life. He then moved from ICI to BOC Ltd to become Gases Division Personnel Manager, where he integrated the OD role within the total personnel function and helped to bring about a division-wide change programme. His most recent move, to Director of Personnel with the Babcock Power and Process Engineering Group, has involved him in the problems of the power engineering industry and in the massive changes which it is undergoing.

Dean Wilson Corporate Manpower Adviser to Reed International. He previously worked in the air transport and food industries and in educational technology. Dean Wilson now specializes in the selection and development of managers and management teams.

References

1 TOFFLER A, *Future Shock*, Random House, 1970
2 LAWRENCE P R and LORSCH J W, *Organization and Environment*, Richard D Irwin, 1967
3 STEELE F, Is Organization Development Work Possible in the UK Culture? *Journal of European Training*, Vol 5 No 3, 1976, p 107
4 SCHEIN E H, *Process Consultation: Its Role in Organization Development*, Addison-Wesley, 1969, p 11
5 KELLY J, *Organizational Behaviour*, Richard D Irwin, 1969
6 TOWNSEND R, *Up the Organization*, Coronet Books, 1971, p 123
7 MCGREGOR D, *The Human Side of Enterprise*, McGraw-Hill, 1960
8 PATTEN T H and VAILL P B, Organization Development, *Training and Development Handbook: A Guide to Human Resource Development*, ed by R L Craig, McGraw-Hill, 1976, pp 20–8
9 COOPER C L and NOBO KUNIYA, *Participative Management Practice and Work Humanization in Japan*, Occasional Paper No 1, Work Research Unit, Department of Employment, 1977, p 8
10 MAYO E, *The Human Problems of an Industrial Civilization*, Macmillan, 1933
11 LEWIN K, *Group Decision and Social Change, Readings in Social Psychology*, ed by T Newcomb and E Hartley, Holt, 1947
12 CAMPBELL J P and DUNNETTE M D, Effectiveness of T-Group Experiences in Managerial Training and Development, *Psychological Bulletin*, Vol 70 No 2 1968, pp 73–104
13 DEWEY J, *The Child and the Curriculum and the School and Society*, University of Chicago Press, 1956
14 ROGERS C, *On Becoming a Person*, Harper and Row, 1970
15 ARGYRIS C, *Intervention Theory and Method*, Addison-Wesley, 1970
16 MCGREGOR D, *op cit*
17 MASLOW A H, *Motivation and Personality*, Harper and Bros, 1970
18 LIKERT R, *New Patterns of Management*, McGraw-Hill, 1961
19 KELLY J, *op cit*
20 MURRAY H, *An Introduction to Sociotechnical Systems at the Level of the Primary Work Group*, Tavistock Institute of Human Relations, 1970
21 CARBY K A, *Job Redesign in Practice*, IPM, 1976, p 62
22 LAWRENCE P R and LORSCH J W, *op cit*
23 BECKHARD R, *Organization Development: Strategies and Models*, Addison-Wesley, 1969
24 BENNIS W G, *Organization Development: Its Nature, Origins and Prospects*, Addison-Wesley, 1969
25 SCHEIN E H, *op cit*
26 LIEVEGOED B C, *The Developing Organization*, translated by J Collis, Tavistock, 1973
27 LAWRENCE P R and LORSCH J W, *Developing Organizations: Diagnosis and Action*, McGraw-Hill, 1969, p 19

28 PATTEN T H and VAILL P B, *op cit*

29 BENNIS W G, *op cit*, p 12

30 SCHMUCK R A and MILES M B, *Organization Development in Schools*, University Associates, 1971

31 SCHEIN E H, *op cit*, p 9

32 *ibid*

33 LAWRENCE P R and LORSCH J W, *op cit*, p 20

34 PATTEN T H and VAILL P B, *op cit*, pp 20–8

35 BENNIS W G, *op cit*, p 17

36 SCHMUCK R A and MILES M B, *op cit*

37 THAKUR M, OD: *The Search for Identity*, IPM, 1974, p 47

38 *ibid* p 50

39 DRAKE R I and SMITH P J, *Behavioural Sciences in Industry*, McGraw-Hill 1972 p 68

40 *ibid* p 70

41 CLARK J V and KRONE C G, Towards an Overall View of Organization Development in the Early Seventies, in *Management of Change and Conflict*, ed by J M Thomas and W G Bennis, Penguin Books, 1972, p 291

42 *ibid*, p 290

43 REDDIN W J, *Managerial Effectiveness*, McGraw-Hill, 1970

44 GILL H S, PEDLER M J and SKIPTON J D, Organization Development and the Trade Unions, *Personnel Review*, Vol 4 No 2, 1975, p 13

45 FOX A, *Sociology of Work in Industry*, Collier-McMillan, 1971

46 PEDLER M J and COOKE P J, Industrial Relations Training in the USA, *Memco* Management Studies Department, Sheffield Polytechnic, 1974, p 76

47 GOODMAN J F B et al, Rules in Industrial Relations Theory: A Discussion, *Industrial Relations Journal*, Vol 6 No 1, 1975

48 MOLLANDER C F, Organization Development and Industrial Relations, *Personnel Review*, Vol 12 No 4, 1973

49 DUNLOP J T, *Industrial Relations Systems*, Holt, Rinehart and Winston, 1958

50 COX R W et al, *Future Industrial Relations: An Interim Report*, International Institute for Labour Studies, Geneva, 1972, pp 3–4

51 ROYAL COMMISSION OF TRADE UNIONS AND EMPLOYERS ASSOCIATIONS, *Donovan Report*, HMSO, 1968

52 MAIER N F, *The Appraisal Interview: Objectives Methods and Skills*, Wiley, 1958

53 KATZ D and KAHN R L, *The Social Psychology of Organizations*, Wiley, 1966

54 HIGGIN G W and BRIDGER H, The Psychodynamics of an Intergroup Experience, *Human Relations*, 17 pp 391–446, Reprinted as Tavistock Pamphlet No 10, 1965

55 BLAKE R R and MOUTON J S, *Building a Dynamic Organization Through Grid Organizational Development*, Addison-Wesley, 1969

56 DEPARTMENT OF HEALTH AND SOCIAL SECURITY, *Management Agreements for the Re-organized National Health Service*, DHSS, 1972 and summarized in NHS Reorganization Circular HRC (73) 3

57 MILLET M, *Approach to Industrial Relations;* unpublished paper to Portsmouth District Health Service District Management Team

58 Taken from the preamble to the Course Programme for the Portsmouth and South East Hants Health District Employee Relations Workshops

59 MINTZBERG H, *The Nature of Managerial Work*, Harper and Row, 1973

60 BLAKE R R and MOUTON J S, *The Managerial Grid*, Gulf Publishing Co, 1964

61 HUMBLE J, *Management by Objectives in Action*, McGraw-Hill, 1970

62 BENNIS W G, *Changing Organizations*, McGraw-Hill, 1966, pp 13–14